ORIGINAL AUDITION SCENES FOR ACTORS

A collection of professional-level short scenes

by
GARRY MICHAEL KLUGER

MERIWETHER PUBLISHING LTD.
COLORADO SPRINGS, COLORADO

6/05

6-30-10
Missing pgs 101-2

Meriwether Publishing Ltd., Publisher
P.O. Box 7710
Colorado Springs, CO 80933

Designer: Michelle Zapel Gallardo
Editor: Arthur Zapel
Typographer: Sharon Garlock

© Copyright MCMLXXXVII Meriwether Publishing Ltd.
Printed in the United States of America
First Edition

Library of Congress Cataloging-in-Publication Data

Kluger, Garry Michael, 1955-
    Original audition scenes for actors.

    1. Acting—Auditions.   I. Title.
PN2071.A92K58 1987   812'.54   87-61894
ISBN 0-916260-45-3

DEDICATION

This book is dedicated to actors and actresses everywhere who have ever had to prepare a scene for an audition.

I would like to thank the following people who have helped the characters in these following pages come to life:

Julie Dolan
Mary Ingersol
Sarah Kendall
Betty Murphy
Ron Preston
Roger Fiets
Ted Warren
Jeanette O'Connor
Jeff Austin
Randy Crowder
Seenwork
Michael Swan
Bruce Kluger
Bernadette Bowman
Dawn Jeffory
Loren Lester
Kathy Talbot
Barney McGeary
Scott Colomby
Helen Baines Colomby
Kim Holman
Cliff Scott

and a very special thank you to **Mr. Bobby Hoffman** *who gives a struggling writer the confidence to continue.*

INTRODUCTION

Once upon a time I told a young actor — "If you can't find a scene for your specific talents, **write one!**" He did. He wrote another, and another, and another! Every scene was different and every scene worked.

I first met Garry Kluger when I was casting ABC-TV's *Happy Days, Laverne & Shirley,* and *Mork & Mindy.* I found him to be an exceptional young actor. He is also, in my opinion, an exceptional young writer. I have attended showcases where Garry's material has been used and I have produced showcases using a great many of the scenes in this book. They are funny, poignant, and above all, excellent material.

I feel Garry's scenes would be ideal for actors for auditioning and showcasing. As casting director for ABC-TV Daytime, I prefer scenes to general interviews. In drama it is almost required to have a scene or monolog. In comedy it is essential.

I feel that I found Garry Kluger, the actor. Now, I am proud to endorse **Garry Kluger, the writer.**

Bobby Hoffman
West Coast Representative,
ABC-TV Daytime
Also formerly casting for *Happy Days,*
Laverne & Shirley, Mork & Mindy, and
Joanie Loves Chachie

Author's Notes

The scenes you are about to read are all a product of my sometimes slightly warped view of life. The scenes themselves have all been performed at showcases and theatres. They have been used to audition actors and actresses at two major networks and have helped many actors to secure jobs. This is my way of saying that my scenes have been widely accepted in professional acting circles.

I am writing this introduction because I want the actors and actresses who use these scenes to be aware of some things I feel are important about the material.

The most important is that a number of the scenes, even though they are written for certain genders, do not have to be performed that way. An example to show this is *Final Exam I* and *Final Exam II*. They are essentially the same scene, but you see that it can be performed two different ways. This should add a lot of versatility to the scenes and some challenges to the actor. The following list of scenes, with certain name and gender reference changes, can be performed in many different combinations. They are:

> *The Awakening, Editor in Chief, Mother, The Drawing Room, The Story, The Politician, The Mixer, The Adult, The Rock Star, The Reporter.*

My second reason for these notes is a personal observance. Though there are several good drama scenes in this book, my favorite type of writing is comedy. I want to say that performing comedy should always be enjoyable. Find ways to have a lot of fun when doing these scenes. If you enjoy performing the scenes, the audience will enjoy watching them.

Enjoy this book and good luck to all.

Garry Kluger

TABLE OF CONTENTS

NOTE: *The numerals running vertically down the left margin of each page of dialog are for the convenience of the director. With these, he/she may easily direct attention to a specific passage.*

PART 1:
COMEDY SCENES

The Awakening

CAST: Sandy — mid 20s; Jo — mid 20s.

SCENE OPENS: Sandy is seated in a chair in the make-up room. Sandy is about twenty-five years old. She is an actress, very famous. It is about five-thirty in the morning. She is waiting for her hair and make-up artist. Not only is she tired, but she is not in the best mood.

ENTER JO: She is about the same age as Sandy. Jo is one of the top people in her field. She is Sandy's personal make-up artist. Why she stays with Sandy is a mystery, but they are friends.

JO: *(Coming up behind)* **Good morning Sandy, isn't it beautiful out today? So clear, so clean.**

SANDY: **Stick it, Jo!**

JO: **Ah, charming as ever I see. What's the matter, get out of the wrong side of the bed this morning?**

SANDY: **I don't know, it wasn't my bed. I didn't know which side was right.**

JO: **Out playing again? Well that explains it.**

SANDY: **Explains what?**

JO: **Why you look terrible.**

SANDY: **Thank you very much. There happens to be a very good reason why I look like this.**

JO: **What's that?**

SANDY: **I had to get up at the obscene hour of five a.m.**

JO: **What's so obscene about five a.m.?**

SANDY: **You have to understand, *God* created five a.m. to come home at, not get up at.**

JO: **Where did you hear that?**

SANDY: **I don't remember. I think it was on Sermonette.**

(They both start to laugh. JO then gets out some of her make-up and starts to work on SANDY'S eyes.)

SANDY: **What are you doing?**

1   JO: I thought I would start on your eyes first today since we
2   had so much trouble with them yesterday.
3   SANDY: *We* didn't have any trouble yesterday, *you* just used
4   too much shadow.
5   JO: I did no such thing.
6   SANDY: Come on Jo, I had more eye make-up on yesterday
7   than Michael Jackson.
8   JO: *Fine!* (She takes off what she has done and starts over.) Let
9   me ask you a question.
10 SANDY: What?
11 JO: Why are you such a flat note?
12 SANDY: *(Pause)* People keep saying that.
13 JO: Like who?
14 SANDY: Aside from you, husbands two and three.
15 JO: What about husband number one?
16 SANDY: He never called me a witch till after the divorce.
17 JO: Maybe there's something in what we've all said.
18 SANDY: You know, if you weren't one of the best at what
19   you do, you'd never be able to get away with that.
20 JO: Thank you, but I must correct you about something. I'm
21   not one of the best, I am the best. *(She continues to work on*
22   *SANDY'S hair.)*
23 SANDY: Jo, could you stop for a minute and sit down?
24 JO: What is it?
25 SANDY: What you said a minute ago, is it true?
26 JO: Is what true?
27 SANDY: Am I really a flat note?
28 JO: Well, *(Pause)* sometimes.
29 SANDY: You didn't think too long about that.
30 JO: You asked me and I feel that we know each other well
31   enough to tell the truth. *(Pause)* Why did you ask?
32 SANDY: I don't know, maybe I'm just feeling insecure.
33 JO: Insecure about what?
34 SANDY: About nothing, about everything.
35 JO: I don't understand, you're doing great, your films are

1   doing well, you're famous and well known . . .
2   SANDY: *(Interrupting)* Yeah, but for how long?
3   JO: Sandy, this is a side of you I've never seen. What brought
4   this on?
5   SANDY: Well, I got home from the set the other night, alone,
6   and I started thinking. What if all this just ends. You
7   know, an actress can be hot one minute and unknown
8   the next. *(Pause)* I don't know why I started thinking
9   about this. You know how it is when you're alone.
10   JO: *(Thinking)* I think the key word here is alone. Is that
11   what this is really all about? Is this why you're so sour
12   and why you keep fooling around?
13   SANDY: *(Starting to tear.)* I guess so. Ever since I got famous
14   I don't know who my friends are. Also, I don't know if a
15   guy likes *me* or who he see's on the screen. Maybe it's
16   why I tend to be abrasive. I know it's why my marriages
17   didn't work.
18   JO: It sounds like you've been doing a little soul searching.
19   You ought to keep it up. It's not a bad thing. You have a
20   tendency to push a little, but there's really no reason to.
21   Loosen up, let some people in. There is an incredible
22   person in there that you should let more people see. Let
23   her out. You're smart enough to separate the cream from
24   the crap. You have a lot more friends than you think.
25   Also, when you meet that right guy, you'll know.
26   SANDY: Jo, are you my friend?
27   JO: Of course I am. That's one you don't have to worry about.
28   *(She gives SANDY a hug.)* Besides, if I weren't your friend
29   I would have already told the *National Enquirer* your
30   real name is Thelma Gritch. Now, let's get back to your
31   eyes before you cry off all your make-up.
32   SANDY: *(SANDY leans back and closes her eyes.)* OK, but not
33   too much shadow. *(They both start to laugh.)*
34   END
35

Editor In Chief

3 **CAST:** Billy — mid 20s; Joyce — mid 20s.

4 **SCENE OPENS:** Billy Preston is sitting in his apartment. He is
5 reading the paper and drinking a cup of coffee. He is in his
6 twenties and is a reporter. Someone starts knocking loudly at
7 his door.

9 **JOYCE:** *(Offstage)* **Billy, are you in there? Billy I know that**
10 **you're in there. Open this door!**

11 **BILLY:** *(Yelling)* **It's open Joyce. Come on in.** *(JOYCE enters.*
12 *She is also in her twenties. She owns the magazine that BILLY*
13 *works for. As she enters it is apparent that she is very mad.)* **Hi**
14 **Joyce, how are you?**

15 **JOYCE:** **Don't you "Hi Joyce" me, you pinhead. Where the**
16 **hell have you been for the last three days?**

17 **BILLY:** **Pinhead? Has anyone ever told you that you have**
18 **all the charm of a rattlesnake?**

19 **JOYCE:** **Kiss my butt.**

20 **BILLY:** **Oh good, that's better.**

21 **JOYCE:** **Look, are you going to tell me where you've been or**
22 **not?**

23 **BILLY:** **Yes, I'll tell you, but first sit down before your ulcer**
24 **acts up.**

25 **JOYCE:** **That's pretty funny coming from you since you're**
26 **the one who gave it to me.** *(She sits.)*

27 **BILLY:** **That's better. Can I get you a cup of coffee?**

28 **JOYCE:** *(Through clenched teeth)* **Thank you.**

29 **BILLY:** *(BILLY gets up and goes to the table. He gets a second cup*
30 *and goes back to the couch and hands it to JOYCE.)* **I think**
31 **you'll like this. I just made it.** *(He then pours half of his cup*
32 *into hers.)* **Cheers.** *(He drinks. She looks at him then puts her*
33 *cup down.)*

34 **JOYCE:** **You're repulsive.**

35 **BILLY:** **You know, since you've come in here, you've called**

1   me a pinhead, repulsive and told me to kiss your butt.
2   Would I be correct in assuming that your ticked at me?
3   JOYCE: Knock if off Billy. When you stormed out of my office
4   the other day you were so mad that it scared me. Then
5   when I couldn't get a hold of you for three days . . .
6   BILLY: (Cutting her off.) You decided to find me. Well, if it
7   makes you feel any better I've been here the whole time.
8   JOYCE: (Getting mad.) Here? Here? I've been worried sick for
9   the last three days and you've been here?
10   BILLY: Yeah. When I have a problem I like to come home,
11   unplug the phone and think till I figure out what to do.
12   JOYCE: Well, what have you decided. Are you still going to
13   quit?
14   BILLY: That depends. Are you still going to kill my story
15   idea for next month's issue?
16   JOYCE: I'm afraid so.
17   BILLY: Then, yes.
18   JOYCE: Well, I guess we have nothing to talk about then.
19   BILLY: I guess not.
20   JOYCE: Fine then, I'm leaving. (She starts to leave.)
21   BILLY: Joyce, what happened to you? (This stops her at the
22   door.)
23   JOYCE: What's that supposed to mean?
24   BILLY: Nothing.
25   JOYCE: No, tell me Billy.
26   BILLY: OK, it just seems that you've changed a lot lately.
27   JOYCE: How.
28   BILLY: I don't know. I just remember when we started
29   reporting for your father a couple of years ago we were
30   going to turn this magazine into something more than
31   third rate. We wanted people to buy it because it was
32   good, not because Time and Newsweek were sold out.
33   JOYCE: And we've done that. Since my father died and I
34   took over, our circulation is up. We're getting more
35   advertisers.

1 BILLY: But at what cost. Look at the garbage we're writing
2   about.
3 JOYCE: That's not fair. Just because we're not doing the
4   dribble that you want to do, doesn't make it garbage.
5 BILLY: Dribble? "The Victims of Gang Violence" is dribble?
6   Where did you study journalsim, at *Sears?*
7 JOYCE: OK, maybe that's the wrong word, but it's nothing
8   new. It's not current.
9 BILLY: *Not current?* It's on the news every night. It's a real
10   problem that should be reported on.
11 JOYCE: That's just it. People get tired of reading about the
12   same things. We need new and exciting stories.
13 BILLY: Oh, I see. And I suppose that our last cover story,
14   "Madonna's 101 Ways To A Better Cocktail Party" is up
15   for a Pulitzer?
16 JOYCE: You just don't understand. I have other
17   responsibilities now. I have a staff that has to be paid
18   and advertisers to make happy. I have to make sure this
19   magazine doesn't go under. It's a business ~~goddamn it,~~
20   not a hobby. I have to approve everything and I don't
21   have the time to discuss everything with you like I used
22   to.
23 BILLY: The great American cop-out, it's a business. So, while
24   you sell out, I'm left to be the moral and social conscience
25   of this magazine, trying to raise it's standards by myself.
26 JOYCE: *(Taking a pause.)* You know something, you are a
27   pretentious, self-centered, egotistical little putz.
28 BILLY: Now wait a minute, I resent that statement.
29 JOYCE: Do you deny it?
30 BILLY: No, but I resent it.
31 JOYCE: *(JOYCE laughs a little, breaking the tension.)* **Look Billy,**
32   **I don't want you to quit. I need you at the magazine.**
33   **You're my friend and I value your opinion.**
34 BILLY: Plus, I'm the best reporter you've got.
35 JOYCE: I know.

1 BILLY: You know?
2 JOYCE: Of course I do, but you've got to work with me.
3   Sometimes you have to go along with my decisions
4   without question.
5 BILLY: Good luck. *(Pause)* Do me a favor — read it. *(He takes*
6   *out an article and hands it to her.)*
7 JOYCE: Billy, we've been through this.
8 BILLY: *Read!*
9 JOYCE: *(She does, begrudgingly. Then slows down as she reads.)*
10   This is good.
11 BILLY: I know.
12 JOYCE: OK, I'll make a deal. I'll read it and we'll discuss it,
13   *if* you'll come back to work.
14 BILLY: OK, sounds fair.
15 JOYCE: I'll expect you at the office at one.
16 BILLY: I can't make it till two.
17 JOYCE: One-thirty.
18 BILLY: Deal.
19   *(She exits.)*
20   **END**
21
22
23
24
25
26
27
28
29
30
31
32
33
34
35

The Wedding

CAST: Tricia — early 20s; Stacy — early 20s.

SCENE OPENS: We are in the waiting room of a church, before a wedding. Tricia is pacing very nervously. She is obviously the bride-to-be. Coming in is Stacy. She is Tricia's sister. She is not at all nervous.

TRICIA: Where the hell have you been?

STACY: At my apartment, where do you think?

TRICIA: Well, you should have been here hours ago.

STACY: Tricia, it's only eight-thirty. The wedding isn't going on for about four hours. If I got here any earlier, I would have beaten the Nuns to the church.

TRICIA: Well, I still think it would have been more considerate if you had gotten here earlier.

STACY: *Considerate!* You're talking about being considerate. Who called who at two a.m. to ask if I remembered everything I had to do.

TRICIA: I apologized for that, didn't I?

STACY: Sure, but you did it again at three, four and five. *Plus*, do you remember what you wanted me to do at six?

TRICIA: No, *(Pause)* what?

STACY: You wanted me to come over and press your dress and do your hair.

TRICIA: Did you?

STACY: No. I managed to get two hours of sleep. Then I came over here. Now, what's wrong with you?

TRICIA: *Nothing!* I'm perfectly fine.

STACY: Sure you are. Do you know even your hair is tense?

TRICIA: OK, so I'm a little nervous.

STACY: A little? I've heard that convicts walking the last mile are calmer than you.

TRICIA: That's an interesting analogy. I *feel* like I'm walking the last mile.

1	STACY:	Why?
2	TRICIA:	*Because I'm getting married!*
3	STACY:	Will you sit down, please. *(TRICIA sits.)* **Now, let me**
4		**explain something to you. You are marrying a great guy.**
5		**David's successful, he's good looking and most**
6		**importantly, he loves you and you love him.**
7	TRICIA:	*(TRICIA ponders this while STACY comes up behind her*
8		*and starts brushing her hair.)* **Yeah, I guess you're right.**
9	STACY:	I know I'm right.
10	TRICIA:	Stacy, you know what I've been thinking about.
11	STACY:	No, what?
12	TRICIA:	You remember when we were kids and we'd talk
13		about our weddings?
14	STACY:	I'm not sure.
15	TRICIA:	Sure you do. Remember, we'd play beauty parlor.
16		One of us would be the hair stylist and the other would
17		be the customer.
18	STACY:	That's right. As we washed our hair the other would
19		tell about the plans for their wedding.
20	TRICIA:	What was so funny is that, as I think back, this
21		wedding is the same as my fantasy.
22	STACY:	Almost the same.
23	TRICIA:	What's different?
24	STACY:	If I remember correctly, you said you were going to
25		be married at Buckingham palace.
26	TRICIA:	So there's one little discrepency. Everything else is
27		the same. *(STACY starts to laugh.)* **What's so funny?**
28	STACY:	Do you remember the time I was the hair dresser
29		and you were the customer and you told me you were
30		going to marry Brad Hurst.
31	TRICIA:	How could I forget. You had a crush on him and
32		when I said I was going to marry him, you gave me a
33		crew cut and dyed my hair blue.
34	STACY:	If you had left it, you'd be right in fashion these
35		days. Besides, I think it looked great.

1   TRICIA: Too bad Mom didn't think so. She spanked you so
2   hard you didn't sit down for a week.
3   STACY: A week? Do you know when I could sit down
4   comfortably?
5   TRICIA: No, when?
6   STACY: Yesterday. *(They both laugh.)* I still can't believe
7   you're really getting married today.
8   TRICIA: I can. Nobody throws up three times in an hour
9   unless they're getting married or are pregnant. So since
10   I'm definitely not pregnant, by process of elimination I
11   must be getting married. *(They laugh again.)*
12   STACY: OK, aside from being nervous, how do you really feel.
13   TRICIA: Stacy, it's hard to explain. Ever since I met David,
14   I knew he was something special. I think about being
15   with someone for a long time and I know there is nobody
16   else I want to spend my life with.
17   STACY: That's sound nice.
18   TRICIA: You know what the best part is?
19   STACY: No, what?
20   TRICIA: I really love him.
21   STACY: Oh, that's good. It's so much easier when you do.
22   TRICIA: You know what I mean. A lot of people say they're
23   in love, but David and I really are. I know this is going
24   to work.
25   STACY: You know, when you talk like this I get really
26   jealous. I'd love to find someone like that.
27   TRICIA: Come on honey, you will.
28   STACY: Oh, there's something I want you to wear.
29   TRICIA: What? *(STACY gets up and gets a box and gives it to*
30   *TRICIA.)*
31   STACY: I know you have something old, and something blue.
32   Here, this is the borrowed one.
33   TRICIA: *(TRICIA opens the box.)* Oh my God, it's the broach
34   Grandma gave you when you were a baby. I can't.
35   STACY: Please, I really want you to wear it.

1	TRICIA: *Really?* You always told me if I touched this you
2	would cut my fingers off. Thanks. You'll get it back after
3	the wedding. *(She gives STACY a big hug.)*
4	STACY: Look we have to start getting ready, but I want to
5	tell you something.
6	TRICIA: What?
7	STACY: I want you to know that not only are you my little
8	sister, but you're the best friend I've ever had. I am so
9	exicted for you and I hope that you will get everything
10	you've wanted. You just make sure that David knows how
11	lucky he is.
12	TRICIA: Thanks.
13	STACY: Also, if you ever need anyone to talk to, just call.
14	You know where you can find me. I love you very much.
15	TRICIA: I love you too. *(They hug once more.)*
16	STACY: There is one thing though.
17	TRICIA: What?
18	STACY: If you are having problems, call in the morning,
19	*please. (They both laugh.)*
20	**END**
21	
22	
23	
24	
25	
26	
27	
28	
29	
30	
31	
32	
33	
34	
35	

The Funeral

CAST: Lucy — 40s; Shellye — 20s.

SCENE OPENS: We are at the funeral for Sam Hoff. Seated is Lucy. She was Sam's wife. She is in her late thirties, early forties. She is crying or at least trying to make an attempt at it. Enter Shellye. She is in her mid to late twenties. She was Sam's niece. She sits down, pulls out some tissue and starts her crying routine.

LUCY: *(Noticing who is sitting next to her.)* **I guess the ghouls come out at funerals.**

SHELLYE: *(SHELLYE stops crying and notices who is next to her.)* **Well, hello Aunt Lucy. I'm surprised to see you here.**

LUCY: Why? Didn't you think I'd show up at my own husband's funeral?

SHELLYE: Yes, but I didn't think the Betty Ford clinic would let you out till your treatments were finished.

LUCY: Witty as usual. Tell me dear, did you come alone or did you bring one of your tricks?

SHELLYE: OK, I can see where this is heading, so why don't we cool it. This *is* a funeral.

LUCY: Yes it is and since funerals are usually attended by people with manners, grace and class, whatever possessed *you* to attend?

SHELLYE: If you must know, I came to pay my respects to my favorite uncle.

LUCY: Favorite my foot. You never cared about him when he was alive, why all the concern now?

SHELLYE: That's not true. He was warm, He was kind. He was . . .

LUCY: *(Interrupting)* **Rich!**

SHELLYE: This all sounds pretty funny coming from the person who killed him.

LUCY: That's a horrible lie!

1   SHELLYE: Really? Wasn't it true that when Uncle Sam came
2   to you complaining of chest pains, you told him it was
3   probably a cold.
4   LUCY: I said that, but when things got worse I called the
5   paramedics.
6   SHELLYE: Before or after he stopped breathing?
7   LUCY: That's it! *(She stands up, throws her purse down, faces*
8   *SHELLYE and starts yelling.)* OK, listen up. This is a funeral
9   and I would like to bury my husband with some peace
10   and dignity if that's all right with you, you cheap broad.
11   SHELLYE: *(SHELLYE looks around.)* A little louder dear, I
12   don't think they heard you in New Jersey.
13   LUCY: *(LUCY looks around, a little embarrassed, sits and composes*
14   *herself.)* Why don't you leave. Nobody wants you here.
15   SHELLEY: Actually Bruce Marshall told me to come.
16   LUCY: Sam's lawyer, why?
17   SHELLYE: I don't know. He said that he wanted to talk to
18   me after the service.
19   LUCY: Wait a minute, I know why. It has to do with the
20   reading of the will tomorrow.
21   SHELLYE: *(Getting concerned.)* What, tell me.
22   LUCY: *(Starting to smile.)* I'm sure he wants to warn you that
23   if you're in the will, I plan to contest it.
24   SHELLYE: *(Stands up and yells.)* You wouldn't! *(She notices*
25   *people are watching. She sits.)* You wouldn't.
26   LUCY: Don't bet on it. You forgot that five years ago I gave
27   you a piece of advice.
28   SHELLYE: What was that?
29   LUCY: I reminded you that you may be his niece, but I sleep
30   with him, so don't mess with me.
31   SHELLYE: Trust me, I remember that.
32   LUCY: Then you didn't heed my warning, so now you have
33   to pay.
34   SHELLYE: What grounds do you plan to contest the will on?
35   LUCY: I'm not sure, but with your past I have a large variety

1   of sleazy items to choose from.
2 SHELLYE: Maybe I'll have to cause some problems of my
3   own.
4 LUCY: About what?
5 SHELLYE: About marrying Sam for his money.
6 LUCY: That's ridiculous.
7 SHELLYE: Is it? Then explain why you married an eighty-
8   seven-year-old man, *only* after finding out he had a bad
9   heart, bad lungs, and has been impotent since 1947.
10 LUCY: OK, you know why I married the old buzzard and so
11   do I, but try and bring it out and all it will look like is
12   the jealous niece against the grieving widow. You don't
13   stand a chance. *(She laughs.)*
14 SHELLYE: That stinks.
15 LUCY: Yes it does. So why don't you slink out the way you
16   came in. *(LUCY gets up and starts to leave.)*
17 SHELLYE: Where are you going? To Rico? *(This stops LUCY*
18   *in her tracks. She goes back to her seat.)*
19 LUCY: *(Nervous)* Who was that?
20 SHELLYE: Rico.
21 LUCY: I don't know who you're talking about.
22 SHELLYE: You don't? He's been your gardner for five years.
23   You know, tall, good looking. *(Pause)* Drives a Rolls. You
24   must pay him very well.
25 LUCY: You can't prove a thing.
26 SHELLYE: I'm afraid I can. *(She pulls some photos from her*
27   *purse.)* When you gave me that warning I decided to keep
28   my eye and *(Pause)* other things focused on you. *(She gives*
29   *the photos to LUCY.)* That Little Bo-Peep outfit really isn't
30   very flattering. You can keep those, I have lots of copies.
31 LUCY: What do you want?
32 SHELLYE: Leave my inheritance alone.
33 LUCY: And if I refuse?
34 SHELLYE: Then these photos will have more circulation
35   than the *New York Times.*

1 LUCY: That's extortion!
2 SHELLYE: Lucy, Lucy, extortion is such an ugly word.
3 LUCY: Then what would you call it?
4 SHELLYE: Oh, I call it extortion, but it's such an ugly word.
5 LUCY: I don't have a choice, do I?
6 SHELLYE: No.
7 LUCY: Fine. You'll have no problem with me.
8 SHELLYE: I knew you'd see it my way. It's always so nice to
9   see you *dear*. (SHELLYE gets up and leaves. LUCY watches
10   her.)
11 LUCY: *Witch!*
12   (Lights out)
13   **END**
14
15
16
17
18
19
20
21
22
23
24
25
26
27
28
29
30
31
32
33
34
35

An Acting Experience

CAST: Adam — mid 20s; Jillian — early 20s.

SCENE OPENS: We are in a living room. Adam is seated on the couch reading the paper. Jillian enters, just back from an audition. She stands by the end of the couch very tight lipped. Also, very mad. Adam looks up.

ADAM: **Hi.** *(JILLIAN, without saying a word, looks at him. She takes her shoulder bag off and sets in on the floor. She looks to ADAM, takes the bag and kicks it across the floor. She then throws her script down and screams a frustrated scream, very loudly. ADAM waits till she is done.)* **I take it the audition didn't go well.**

JILLIAN: **Go to hell!**

ADAM: **Ah, that good!**

JILLIAN: *(JILLIAN starts to pace as she speaks.)* **What does he know, anyway?**

ADAM: **Who?**

JILLIAN: **Who do you think? If I ever see that little putz again I'm going to rip his . . . He'll wish he'd never heard my name . . . He'll . . .**

ADAM: **OK, OK, calm down.**

JILLIAN: **But he . . .**

ADAM: **But he nothing, calm down.** *(Pause)* **That's better. Now sit. Tell me what happened.**

JILLIAN: **Well, I went into this office and was introduced to this slug who calls himself a director. He told me I wasn't right and he wouldn't let me read.**

ADAM: **Why?**

JILLIAN: **I don't know.**

ADAM: **OK, let me see the script, and maybe we can both figure it out.**

JILLIAN: **Fine.** *(She gets up and picks up script from the floor. It has been squished into a ball. She gives it to him and sits down*

1   *next to him.)*
2   ADAM: What were you reading for.
3   JILLIAN: Mary. She comes in on page seventeen.
4   ADAM: Mary?
5   JILLIAN: *Mary!*
6   ADAM: Mary. *(ADAM reads the script, stops looks at JILLIAN*
7   *and then proceeds to read aloud from the script.)* **"Mary enters.**
8   **She is a young pretty girl. She is approximately seventeen**
9   **years old and black."** Did your agent send you out for this?
10   JILLIAN: No, Judy Lloyd read for it and she told me about it.
11   ADAM: Judy Lloyd is black.
12   JILLIAN: It doesn't matter. I'm a better actress than she is.
13   ADAM: But she's *black!*
14   JILLIAN: I *don't care!* I can play that part. I've been to
15   Strasberg's. I've been to the Actor's Studio. *(Proudly)* I can
16   run on stage naked.
17   ADAM: And I suppose you told him that.
18   JILLIAN: Of course.
19   ADAM: Of course. Jilly, I think you're missing the . . . .
20   JILLIAN: *(Cutting him off.)* Wait a minute. Do you think he
21   treated me fairly? Would you have done that to me?
22   ADAM: Me, no. I would have had you committed.
23   JILLIAN: *(Indignant)* Why?
24   ADAM: Because you're crazy, that's why.
25   JILLIAN: I should have known better than to talk to you.
26   You have no sensitivity or understanding?
27   ADAM: I have no sensitivity or understanding?
28   JILLIAN: You got it!
29   ADAM: You want to know what it's like living with you and
30   your career. No don't answer. I'll tell you. It's like living
31   with Sybil. Do you know that in the last week I have
32   made love with Lady Macbeth, Joan of Arc, and Blanche
33   Du Bois. *(JILLIAN starts to say something, but ADAM stops*
34   *her.)* OK, I'll give you that Blanche was fun, but last night
35   was the limit.

1	JILLIAN: Why? I thought it would be exciting.
2	ADAM: Jillian, I didn't want to sleep with King Lear!
3	JILLIAN: Why not? He's royalty, he's got charisma. He's
4	got . . .
5	ADAM: He also has a beard. You're making me question my
6	own sexuality. You're . . . I don't know why I'm talking
7	about this. I don't have a problem, you do. You're not
8	going to work till you change your approach.
9	JILLIAN: How?
10	ADAM: Start telling the truth.
11	JILLIAN: *(Pause)* What?
12	ADAM: Start being honest about yourself.
13	JILLIAN: Honest? With casting people? Are you crazy? No
14	way.
15	ADAM: Why not?
16	JILLIAN: Because I've never done that before. I don't think
17	I even know how.
18	ADAM: Then don't think about it as being honest. Think of
19	it as an acting exercise.
20	JILLIAN: An acting exercise?
21	ADAM: Yeah. *(Searching)* Yeah . . . you know how you are
22	when you're not thinking about the business?
23	JILLIAN: No.
24	ADAM: No. OK, uh . . . you know how you were when we went
25	to Tijuana?
26	JILLIAN: No, yes.
27	ADAM: Well, that's Jillian Carson, real person. Be her. Act
28	like her the next time you have an audition.
29	JILLIAN: Jillian Carson, ordinary person? *(Thinking)* You
30	know, that's crazy enough to work. She's an easy
31	character. Hell, I could probably do her in my sleep.
32	ADAM: That certainly would be a switch.
33	JILLIAN: *(Getting excited.)* Yeah, it'll work. That's a great idea.
34	Why didn't I think of it. Thank you honey. *(ADAM goes*
35	*back to work. JILLIAN picks up a "Variety" and starts miming*

her new approach.)

2 JILLIAN: Hi, I'm Jillian Carson, real person, and I want to
3 give you my picture and resume. No. Hi, I'd like
4 to . . . *(Notices something in the magazine.)* **Oh, my God!**
5 ADAM: What?
6 JILLIAN: They're auditioning "Boys In the Band." I'm
7 perfect for the lead. *(ADAM gets up and leaves the room.*
8 *JILLIAN follows him, talking.)* No Adam, really. I can play
9 gay. All I need is a moustache.
10 END
11
12
13
14
15
16
17
18
19
20
21
22
23
24
25
26
27
28
29
30
31
32
33
34
35

Mother

CAST: Nancy — 30s; Lily — 50s.

SCENE OPENS: We are in a living room. Nancy is on the couch. Nancy is in her thirties. She is burned out and very tired. She has an icepack on her temple. At the door about to enter is her mother, Lily.

LILY: *(Offstage)* **Nancy are you home?** *(Pause)* **Nancy, it's Mom.**

NANCY: **Mom, who?**

LILY: *(LILY enters.)* **What do you mean, "Mom who?" How many Moms do you have?**

NANCY: **Today, none.**

LILY: **Why?**

NANCY: **Because I realized today that no woman would bring a child into this world knowing that someday they might feel like this.**

LILY: **Well, if I must say so, you do look like . . .**

NANCY: **Like dirt, Mom?**

LILY: **I wasn't going to say that.**

NANCY: **But you were thinking it, right?**

LILY: **Not at all. I was going to say that you looked tired.**

NANCY: **I am. What are you doing here?**

LILY: **Oh, I see. I have to have a reason to visit my daughter.**

NANCY: **No you don't. I'm sorry. Do you want a cup of coffee?**

LILY: **Thank you, I would.**

NANCY: **Good, when you get yourself a cup, would you get me one?** *(LILY get's up, goes over and pours two cups. She brings one over to NANCY.)* **Thanks. So, what can I do for you.**

LILY: **Nothing. I was just in the neighborhood, so I thought I'd stop in.**

NANCY: **In the neighborhood? Mother, you live thirty miles away. How did you just happen to be in this neighborhood?**

1   LILY: *(Struggling)* I was shopping at the market.
2   NANCY: Oh, that's right. I forgot they don't have any food
3   where you live. Come on Mother, what's up?
4   LILY: *(LILY sits.)* Well, to be honest, your father and I have
5   been worried about you lately.
6   NANCY: Why, there's no reason to be.
7   LILY: No reason? Look at you, you're exhausted.
8   NANCY: It's Sunday. I'm supposed to be. If you don't believe
9   me, check your Bible.
10 LILY: What's that supposed to mean?
11 NANCY: Right in Genesis it says, "And God created Sunday
12   and he was exhausted."
13 LILY: Will you be serious!
14 NANCY: Will you be. I think I know what this is all about.
15   You and Daddy don't like my life style since I got
16   divorced.
17 LILY: Well, you're right. We don't.
18 NANCY: And what's wrong with it?
19 LILY: For one thing, you're out till all hours. You go out with
20   a lot of different men. In general you're acting like a
21   child. We never see you and we certainly don't know what
22   you're up to.
23 NANCY: And you shouldn't. Mom, I'm over thirty. I don't
24   have to report to you or be in by ten anymore.
25 LILY: Is that any reason to act . . . .act . . .
26 NANCY: Act what?
27 LILY: Loose.
28 NANCY: *(NANCY starts to laugh.)* Loose. Can you expand on
29   that?
30 LILY: You know what I'm talking about.
31 NANCY: No Mother, I don't. Explain.
32 LILY: Where were you last night?
33 NANCY: Here.
34 LILY: Were you alone?
35 NANCY: No.

1	LILY:	What were you doing?
2	NANCY:	Ah, entertaining.
3	LILY:	Entertaining? What does that mean?
4	NANCY:	I was making love. Sex.
5	LILY:	Stop that. Don't use that kind of language. Your father
6		and I never used that word.
7	NANCY:	You never did it either.
8	LILY:	Fine, make jokes. Next I suppose you'll tell me what
9		bad parents we were.
10	NANCY:	I didn't say that, but you were a bit provincial.
11	LILY:	We were not provincial.
12	NANCY:	Oh, come on Mother, because of the way I was
13		brought up I was a virgin till I was twenty-one.
14	LILY:	What's wrong with that?
15	NANCY:	I was married at nineteen.
16	LILY:	Fine, have it your way. Your father and I ruined your
17		life.
18	NANCY:	I didn't say that, but also don't condemn my lifestyle
19		because it's not like yours.
20	LILY:	I'm not condemning.
21	NANCY:	Yes you are.
22	LILY:	Maybe I am, but it's just that Dad and I are worried
23		since your divorce. You don't seem to have any focus. We
24		don't want to see you lonely.
25	NANCY:	Mother, I'm not. Look, for the first time since I was
26		married, I feel good. Work is good, and I'm happy.
27	LILY:	But what about a husband?
28	NANCY:	I had a husband. I was in a bad marriage for over
29		ten years. Now I'm experiencing all those things I couldn't
30		by getting married young.
31	LILY:	Nancy, you are the most precious thing in the world
32		to Dad and me. We only want the best for you. A good
33		job, a husband, and a family.
34	NANCY:	I want that too. I have the job and the others will
35		come in time, but when I'm ready, not before.

```
1   LILY:   Are you really happy?
2   NANCY:   Yes, Mom, I am.
3   LILY:   Well then, that's all that's important. I guess I'll be
4       going. (She gets up, gives NANCY a kiss and starts to leave.)
5   NANCY:   Mom.
6   LILY:   Yes.
7   NANCY:   Stop by, anytime you're here shopping. (They laugh.)
8                   END
9
10
11
12
13
14
15
16
17
18
19
20
21
22
23
24
25
26
27
28
29
30
31
32
33
34
35
```

The Drawing Room

CAST: Samantha — 20s; Brooke — 20s.

SCENE OPENS: Samantha is seated at a table at her apartment. She checks her watch once, then again. Finally she gets up and begins to get ready to go out. She gets her jacket and bag. As she is exiting she runs into Brooke. Brooke is definitely New York up bringing. She has a slight New York accent.

SAMANTHA: Well, it's about time. Another thirty seconds and I would have been gone.

BROOKE: I'm sorry, but as you're always telling me, I'm always a minute short and a day late.

SAMANTHA: That's fine for you, but now you're affecting my whole day. Well, never mind, you're here now. What's so important that I had to give up my aerobics class.

BROOKE: I need a big favor from you.

SAMANTHA: So I gathered from your phone call.

BROOKE: Yeah, I have an audition and I need your help to learn to speak proper.

SAMANTHA: Speak properly!

BROOKE: See, you're the perfect teacher. You can be my Henery Higgins.

SAMANTHA: I'm not sure I appreciate the comparison, but I'll give it a try.

BROOKE: Great! *(She sits at the table.)*

SAMANTHA: First, what's the play and secondly, when's the audition?

BROOKE: The audition is tomorrow and the play is, "The Drawing Room."

SAMANTHA: "The Drawing Room?" Roger Wainright's new play? How did you get an audition for that? I've been trying to get in for that for a month.

BROOKE: My agent showed the director my picture and he told her he wanted to see me.

1   SAMANTHA: I take it he hasn't heard you speak yet?
2   BROOKE: No, he hasn't. That's why I need your help. I figure
3   if anyone can teach me that Roger Wainright, Noel
4   Coward type of stuff, you can.
5   SAMANTHA: What?
6   BROOKE: You know what I mean. All those people in those
7   plays are so uptight. They all walk and talk like they
8   have poles up their butts.
9   SAMANTHA: Brooke, has anyone told you that you have a
10   charming vocabulary?
11   BROOKE: Yeah, my boyfriend.
12   SAMANTHA: Bruno?
13   BROOKE: Yeah.
14   SAMANTHA: It figures.
15   BROOKE: So, are you going to help me, Sammy?
16   SAMANTHA: Not if you call me Sammy.
17   BROOKE: OK, will you help me Samantha?
18   SAMANTHA: Yes I will. I must admit it will be a challenge.
19   BROOKE: Here's the scene I'm reading tomorrow. *(She gives*
20   *SAMANTHA the scripts. She reads it over.)*
21   SAMANTHA: *(In proper British accent)* This is really quite
22   simple.
23   BROOKE: That's great!
24   SAMANTHA: I know. You see, you must remember that these
25   are proper people. It's as if every word they speak is
26   carefully chosen and pronounced.
27   BROOKE: OK, I understand.
28   SAMANTHA: *(Same accent)* Now you are Pamela. Remember
29   what I just told you. Now, how would you say this line?
30   BROOKE: I wouldn't say that line.
31   SAMANTHA: What?
32   BROOKE: I wouldn't say that. Look at this, *(Reading)* "I'm so
33   pleased to make your acquaintance. I hope you're finding
34   your stay a pleasant one." Who talks like that?
35   SAMANTHA: Roger Wainright's people do. What would you

1   say?

2   **BROOKE:**   **I don't know.** *(Pause)* **How about, "Nice to see ya.**

3   **How's it going?"**

4   **SAMANTHA:**   *(Dropping her accent)* **"Nice to see ya, how's it**

5   **going?" You've got to be kidding.**

6   **BROOKE:**   **Why?**

7   **SAMANTHA:**   **Because you're auditioning for Pamela and this is**

8   **how she speaks.**

9   **BROOKE:**   *(Getting angry)* **Well, it's a dumb way to talk and**

10   **I'm not going to do it.**

11   **SAMANTHA:**   **I should have my head examined trying to**

12   **teach proper English to a person with the grammatical**

13   **patterns of Rocky.**

14   **BROOKE:**   **Is that how you feel about it?**

15   **SAMANTHA:**   **Yes.**

16   **BROOKE:**   **Great, why don't we just forget about it then.**

17   **SAMANTHA:**   **That suits me fine.**

18   **BROOKE:**   **Me too, bye.** *(BROOKE picks up her things and starts*

19   *to exit.)*

20   **SAMANTHA:**   **Halt!** *(BROOKE stops at the door.)* **First off, you**

21   **forgot your script.** *(She hands the script back.)* **Secondly, I**

22   **won that argument too easily.**

23   **BROOKE:**   **What are you talking about?**

24   **SAMANTHA:**   **I've known you for a long time Brooke. You**

25   **don't want to do well tomorrow.**

26   **BROOKE:**   **You're crazy.**

27   **SAMANTHA:**   **Am I? Come on Brooke, be straight with me.**

28   **What's wrong?**

29   **BROOKE:**   **I** *am,* **and nothing's wrong!**

30   **SAMANTHA:**   **There is too.**

31   **BROOKE:**   *There is not!*

32   **SAMANTHA:**   **There is too.** *Now tell me!*

33   *BROOKE:*   *All right, I'll tell you.* *(Pause)* **I'm terrified.**

34   **SAMANTHA:**   **Terrified of what?**

35   **BROOKE:**   *(She softens a bit.)* **I've been acting since I was five**

years old, but all the parts I've gotten I could have slept through. Now I've got a chance to stretch myself as an actress and I'm scared that I won't succeed. That I'll be laughed at. If that happens, I don't know if I could take it.

SAMANTHA: Not meaning to minimize your fears, but you're hardly alone. You *may* be laughed at, then again you may be brilliant. You're too good an actress not to try. I think you can do it, but that's not important if you don't think so.

BROOKE: So, you think I should go for it?

SAMANTHA: Absolutely, at least it will stop you from doing plays like "Biker Heaven" for a while. *(They both laugh and BROOKE gives SAMANTHA a hug.)*

BROOKE: I knew you'd be my Henery Higgins.

SAMANTHA: *(They both laugh. SAMANTHA takes the script from BROOKE and opens it. She offers BROOKE a seat.)* Now, *(In an English accent)* "I'm so pleased to make your acquaintance. I hope you're finding your stay a pleasant one." Repeat please. *(BROOKE starts to repeat the sentence.)*

(Lights out.)

END

1

Surprise

2

3   *CAST:*   David — late 20s; Carol — late 20s.

4   *SCENE OPENS:*   We are in the apartment, the living room of David

5   and Carol Hutchins. They are both in their late 20s, early 30s.

6   They are a typical "Yuppie" couple, upward and mobile. As the

7   scene opens Carol is on the couch waiting for David to come

8   home.

9

10   **DAVID:**   **Carol, I'm home.** *(He enters.)* **Hi, Honey.** *(He goes over*

11   *and gives her a kiss.)*

12   **CAROL:**   **How was your day?**

13   **DAVID:**   **Great, just great. I finally closed the Carmichael**

14   **account this afternoon.**

15   **CAROL:**   **That's wonderful. Look David, could I talk to you**

16   **for a minute?**

17   **DAVID:**   *(DAVID is sort of distracted. He is looking for and pulling*

18   *something out of his briefcase.)* **Yeah sure, in a minute.**

19   **CAROL:**   **I mean now.**

20   **DAVID:**   **In a minute. I just got a couple of new software**

21   **programs and I want to run them through the Apple IIC**

22   **and see what pops up.**

23   **CAROL:**   **Couldn't that wait. I want to talk to you about**

24   **something very important.**

25   **DAVID:**   **Sure.** *(He puts the programs down.)* **What's the matter.**

26   **Did something happen at work?**

27   **CAROL:**   **I didn't go to work.**

28   **DAVID:**   **Why, what's wrong? Was there trouble? Were you**

29   **fired?**

30   **CAROL:**   **No, nothing like that.**

31   **DAVID:**   **Then what's wrong?**

32   **CAROL:**   **You remember that I wasn't feeling quite right this**

33   **morning?**

34   **DAVID:**   **Yes.**

35   **CAROL:**   **Well, I called work and told them I wasn't coming**

1		in. Then I went to my doctor and had a full check-up.
2	DAVID:	Doctor? Check-up? Is everything OK?
3	CAROL:	Yes, everything's fine. In fact, everything's great.
4	DAVID:	Then what's so important that we had to talk about?
5	CAROL:	I'm pregnant.
6	DAVID:	*(Stunned)* You're what?
7	CAROL:	I'm pregnant.
8	DAVID:	*(Still stunned)* You're what?
9	CAROL:	I'm pregnant, David. You know, expecting! With
10		child!
11	DAVID:	Thank you. I know what pregnant is, but how?
12	CAROL:	How?
13	DAVID:	Yes, how?
14	CAROL:	David, you have two degrees from two different
15		universities, you're a vice president and you don't know
16		how a woman gets pregnant?
17	DAVID:	Will you stop. How did you let this happen?
18	CAROL:	Me? If I remember you *did* have something to do
19		with it.
20	DAVID:	I know that, but I thought we took all the
21		precautions.
22	CAROL:	Well, nothing's one hundred percent, except
23		abstention and we both decided that was out.
24	DAVID:	But this is impossible.
25	CAROL:	Why is it impossible?
26	DAVID:	Because of this. *(DAVID goes to his briefcase and pulls*
27		*out a chart.)*
28	CAROL:	Oh no, not that damn chart again.
29	DAVID:	Yes and don't call it a damn chart. It's a psychic read
30		out.
31	CAROL:	It's *bull.*
32	DAVID:	It is not.
33	CAROL:	Oh yeah, how many of those things came true?
34	DAVID:	Plenty. Look here. *(DAVID takes the chart over to her.)*
35		My psychic said I'd be married by this date. I was. She

1	said I'd have enough money for a BMW by this date. I
2	did. She also said I'd be a vice president by this year. I am.
3	CAROL: I could have told you all that. First off, we were
4	married before you met Sambo ...
5	DAVID: *(Interrupting)* Simba.
6	CAROL: Simba. Also, anybody who knows you could tell
7	you'd be a success. You're a go-getter. You've always been
8	one.
9	DAVID: That's true, but ...
10	CAROL: But nothing. And to use your own example, look at
11	this chart. Sampson said ...
12	DAVID: *(Mad)* Simba!
13	CAROL: Whatever. She said you weren't supposed to have
14	a child till June 1989. She's two years off.
15	DAVID: That's true. I don't know how she missed that one
16	so badly.
17	CAROL: I do.
18	DAVID: How?
19	CAROL: I just had something more powerful than your
20	psychic.
21	DAVID: What was that?
22	CAROL: A bottle of champagne and silk lingerie.
23	DAVID: *(Pause)* That's true.
24	CAROL: David, why don't you face it. We are going to have
25	a baby.
26	DAVID: I guess I have to, but it's so sudden. We haven't
27	planned. What are we going to do?
28	CAROL: Stop being so worried. Look, we're both working,
29	we have money. I'm ready to raise a child and I believe
30	you are too.
31	DAVID: It's just that I haven't thought about it before.
32	CAROL: Well start.
33	DAVID: But a baby, I .... *(All of a sudden DAVID stops and*
34	*realizes what he has just said. He starts to get excited.)* Did you
35	hear what I said? A baby! We're going to have a baby.

```
1    CAROL:   Really! Where did you hear that?
2    DAVID:   Stop it. I just realized the magnitude of what's
3             happening. We're going to have a baby.
4    CAROL:   How do you feel about it?
5    DAVID:   Incredible, I think. (Pause) Yes, incredible. You really
6             did it.
7    CAROL:   We did it. (DAVID goes over and gives CAROL a hug
8             and a kiss. They hug again. As they do, CAROL tears up the
9             chart behind DAVID'S back.)
10                              END
11
12
13
14
15
16
17
18
19
20
21
22
23
24
25
26
27
28
29
30
31
32
33
34
35
```

The Set Up

CAST: Tommy — age open; Karen — age open.

SCENE OPENS: Tommy enters. He is a young man in his early
twenties. He is dressed is tennis wear or warm-ups. He has an
ice pack on his eye. Following him is Karen. She is about
nineteen- or twenty-years-old. She is also dressed in tennis or
warm-up gear. Tommy sits on the couch.

TOMMY: *(Touching his ice pack)* **Ow, that hurts.**

KAREN: **Tommy, you left this in my car.**

TOMMY: **Thanks.** *(He takes the bag and puts it on the couch.)*

KAREN: **Is there anything else I can do for you?**

TOMMY: **Yeah.**

KAREN: **What?**

TOMMY: *Go home!*

KAREN: **Come on Tommy, how many times do I have to
apologize?**

TOMMY: **A lot. Look, if you didn't know how to play tennis,
why didn't you just say so?**

KAREN: **I know how to play tennis!**

TOMMY: **Really, how long have you been playing?**

KAREN: **Years.**

TOMMY: **Then you should sue the guy who sold you your
racquet and I should sue you for blinding me.**

KAREN: **Stop being such a baby. I only hit you once.**

TOMMY: **I only let you serve once. If I let you serve twice,
I'd probably be doing a Stevie Wonder impression now.**

KAREN: **Never mind. Anyway, what did you think of my
friends, Muffin and Bambi?**

TOMMY: **Why?**

KAREN: **Well, um . . . well, I was thinking if you liked them,
maybe you'd sort of want to ask one of them out.**

TOMMY: **Is that what this is all about? Is that why you
suggested we play tennis with your friends, so you could**

1   try and set me up?
2   KAREN: Yes. If I had told you that's why I wanted to play
3   tennis, would you have gone?
4   TOMMY: No!
5   KAREN: See. Now, didn't you find them nice?
6   TOMMY: Yes, I did.
7   KAREN: Didn't you find them attractive?
8   TOMMY: Yes, I did.
9   KAREN: Don't you want to ask one of them out?
10 TOMMY: No, I don't.
11 KAREN: Why?
12 TOMMY: To start with, between the two of them they had
13   the I.Q. of peas. Do you know that it took them twenty
14   minutes to figure out that the round object they were
15   holding was a tennis ball?
16 KAREN: God, you're so picky. OK, so they didn't go to
17   Harvard.
18 TOMMY: Go there, they couldn't even spell it.
19 KAREN: OK, if you didn't like them, I have someone else I'd
20   like you to meet.
21 TOMMY: No thank you. Just leave me alone.
22 KAREN: No Tommy, you'll like this one. I met her in my
23   Psych class. She's really smart.
24 TOMMY: Really, what's her name?
25 KAREN: Cindy, *(Pause)* but everyone calls her Twinkle.
26 TOMMY: That's it! Twinkle, Muffin, Bambi — why is it that
27   every girl you know sounds like she just walked out of
28   a Disney movie? *(Pause)* Who's next, Sneezy and Doc?
29 KAREN: Well, you should fit in then, Grumpy.
30 TOMMY: Cute. Karen, why are you so interested in my social
31   life?
32 KAREN: Because we've been friends for a long time and I
33   care about you.
34 TOMMY: Do me a favor, care about me a little less. I don't
35   know if my body can survive much more of your concern.

1   KAREN: Enough with the eye already. Answer me one
2   question, will you?
3   TOMMY: No.
4   KAREN: Good, how long has it been since you had a
5   girlfriend?
6   TOMMY: A little while.
7   KAREN: A little while?
8   TOMMY: Yes, a little while.
9   KAREN: Would you define "a little while," please. Does that
10   mean this decade? Tommy, have you had a girlfriend
11   since Nixon was president?
12   TOMMY: Very funny. OK, how about that girl I dated in high
13   school. Maybe I'll call her up and ask her out.
14   KAREN: Who, Susan? I doubt it. She became a nun right
15   after graduation.
16   TOMMY: So, that doesn't mean she won't go out with me.
17   KAREN: See Tommy, this is my point. Look at you. You are
18   a lonely, frustrated, pathetic individual. I just want to
19   help you before you become a lonely, frustrated, pathetic
20   old man.
21   TOMMY: Thank you for that glimpse into the future.
22   KAREN: But I don't want that to be your future. That's why
23   I want to help.
24   TOMMY: OK, Karen, you are my best friend and I understand
25   that you want to help, but I don't want your help. Please,
26   I don't want to meet any more of your friends.
27   KAREN: Why?
28   TOMMY: I have my reasons, but I don't think I can tell you.
29   KAREN: Oh my God, you're gay.
30   TOMMY: I'm not gay.
31   KAREN: Then tell me why.
32   TOMMY: *No!*
33   KAREN: *Tell me!*
34   TOMMY: OK, you want to know why I don't want to meet
35   any more of your friends?

1 **KAREN:** **Yes.** *(TOMMY walks over to her, grabs her and kisses her*
2 *passionately. He let's her go, puts the ice on his eye and exits.*
3 *KAREN watches as he goes, sort of blank faced. After he leaves*
4 *she looks out front and says:)* **Oh, no!**
5 **END**
6
7
8
9
10
11
12
13
14
15
16
17
18
19
20
21
22
23
24
25
26
27
28
29
30
31
32
33
34
35

Final Exam I

CAST: Michael — college age; Jerrry — college age.

SCENE OPENS: Jerry and Michael are in their dorm room studying. Michael is helping Jerry study for the last test of his college career.

JERRY: The sum of the square of the sides is equal to the square of the hyperbola.

MICHAEL: *(Lifting his head from the table.)* **Hypotenuse.**

JERRY: What?

MICHAEL: The sum of the square of the sides is equal to the square of the hypoenuse, not hyperbola. Get it straight.

JERRY: Come on Michael, it's three fifty-two in the morning. If I don't know this now, I never will.

MICHAEL: You've got to know this. If you don't pass this test, you won't pass this course, and if you don't pass this course you won't graduate.

JERRY: It's not that bad.

MICHAEL: Yes it is! Remember, this is a required course you decided not to take till your senior year.

JERRY: I thought it would be easier, so I waited.

MICHAEL: That's what I don't understand. How is it that you made it through twelve years of public school, four years of college, and on the Dean't List, and you never took a simple geometry course?

JERRY: I was sick that day.

MICHAEL: What day?

JERRY: Any day they taught geometry.

MICHAEL: Will you be serious.

JERRY: I am serious. I'm a political science major, what do I care about Pi R square or Pi R triple.

MICHAEL: Cube.

JERRY: What?

MICHAEL: Cube. Anything times itself is squared and

1   anything times itself three times is cubed.
2   JERRY: Michael, *(Pause)* nobody cares.
3   MICHAEL: This college does and if you don't they won't
4   graduate you.
5   JERRY: So.
6   MICHAEL: What do you mean "so"? You've already been
7   accepted to law school. You can't flunk now.
8   JERRY: I can if I want to.
9   MICHAEL: What's the matter with you? In all the time we've
10   been roommates, I've never seen you like this.
11   JERRY: Nothing's wrong with me. Maybe I just don't want
12   to be a lawyer anymore.
13   MICHAEL: Bull, you've wanted to be a lawyer as long as I've
14   known you.
15   JERRY: I just don't want it anymore.
16   MICHAEL: Well, I don't believe you and neither do you.
17   Besides, what do you think your parents would say?
18   JERRY: I don't care what they say.
19   MICHAEL: That came out a little hostile, didn't it.
20   JERRY: *(Mad) No, it didn't!*
21   MICHAEL: My mistake. *(Pause)* Did you have a fight with
22   your parents?
23   JERRY: No.
24   MICHAEL: Are you sure.
25   JERRY: Yes, and don't bring up my damn parents anymore.
26   MICHAEL: Excuse me for mistaking an obviously harmonious
27   relationship for a troubled one.
28   JERRY: I'm sorry. I didn't mean to yell at you. My parents
29   are getting to me.
30   MICHAEL: How?
31   JERRY: Well, everytime I talk to them they keep telling me
32   about law school. I can't take the pressure anymore. I'm
33   not sure if I ever wanted to go to law school.
34   MICHAEL: So, instead of telling them, you flunk out and
35   *bingo*, no problem.

1   JERRY: I guess so.
2   MICHAEL: Why don't you talk to them?
3   JERRY: I can't. They're not like your folks. They let you be
4   what you want to be.
5   MICHAEL: Is there something else you want to be?
6   JERRY: Yeah, but they wouldn't understand.
7   MICHAEL: How do you know unless you tell them. *(Pause)*
8   What is it?
9   JERRY: *(Pause)* A terrorist. *(They both start laughing.)*
10   MICHAEL: No really? Is there something you want that you
11   never told anyone?
12   JERRY: That's just it, I'm not sure anymore.
13   MICHAEL: Maybe it's graduation nerves. A lot of people get
14   them.
15   JERRY: I've thought about that, but I've had these feelings
16   for a long time.
17   MICHAEL: What do you want to do?
18   JERRY: I don't know. I'm very confused.
19   MICHAEL: So, unconfuse yourself.
20   JERRY: How?
21   MICHAEL: What do you want to do right after graduation?
22   Think fast.
23   JERRY: I'd like to go to Europe and see how many countries
24   I can visit.
25   MICHAEL: Tell that to your parents.
26   JERRY: Yeah, I've got a good picture of that.
27   MICHAEL: No, tell them you want to get away for a while.
28   JERRY: What if they say no.
29   MICHAEL: So what? You're twenty-one. You don't need their
30   permission. Take your own money and go. Law school
31   will always be here.
32   JERRY: What happens if I still don't want law school.
33   MICHAEL: Then you'll do something else. Who knows, after
34   a year of Europe, law school might look real good.
35   JERRY: You can't be serious.

```
1    MICHAEL:  Well, it might. Anyway, don't screw up that
2         chance by flunking this test.
3    JERRY:  Back to the hyperbola?
4    MICHAEL:  Hypotenuse.
5    JERRY:  Michael, (Pause) nobody cares.
6                        END
7
8
9
10
11
12
13
14
15
16
17
18
19
20
21
22
23
24
25
26
27
28
29
30
31
32
33
34
35
```

Final Exam II

CAST: Garry — 21; Julie — 20.

SCENE OPENS: Garry and Julie are in Garry's room at school. They are boyfriend, girlfriend. She is helping Garry study for the final exam of his college career. Julie is sitting on the floor, Garry is asleep in a chair.

JULIE: OK, the Pathagorium Therom. *(There is no answer. She notices that GARRY is asleep. She throws a pillow at him.)* Come on, Garry.

GARRY: *(He wakes up suddenly.)* **What?**

JULIE: The Pathagorium Therom.

GARRY: Oh, OK. Don't help me.

JULIE: I wasn't planning to. *(She picks up a water gun and aims it at him as he recites.)*

GARRY: *(Thinking)* The sum of the square of the sides is equal to the square of the ... the ... hyperbola.

JULIE: *(She squirts him.)* Hypotenuse.

GARRY: That's what I said.

JULIE: You said "Hyperbola."

GARRY: What's the difference?

JULIE: The difference is getting it right or getting it wrong. Now get it straight. *(She squirts him again.)*

GARRY: Stop it! Come on, Julie, it's three fifty-two in the morning. If I don't know it now, I never will.

JULIE: You've got to know this. If you don't pass this test, you won't pass the course, and if you don't pass this course, you won't graduate.

GARRY: It's not that bad.

JULIE: Yes it is. This *is* a required course, you know, the one you decided not to take until your senior year.

GARRY: I thought it would be easier so I waited.

JULIE: That's another thing I don't understand. How is it that you made it through twelve years of public school,

1   four years of college and on the Dean's List . . .

2   GARRY: *(Interrupting)* **Twice.**

3   JULIE: **Twice, and never took a simple geometry course?**

4   GARRY: **I was sick that day.**

5   JULIE: *(Pointing gun)* **What day?**

6   GARRY: **Any day they taught geometry.**

7   JULIE: *(Squirting him)* **Would you be serious.**

8   GARRY: **I am. For Christ's sake Julie, I'm a poly-sci major.**

9   **What do I care about Pi R square or Pi R triple?**

10   JULIE: **Cube.**

11   GARRY: **What?**

12   JULIE: **Anything times itself is squared, anything times**

13   **itself three times is cubed.**

14   GARRY: **Julie?**

15   JULIE: **What?**

16   GARRY: **Nobody cares.**

17   JULIE: **This college does, and if you don't, they won't**

18   **graduate you.**

19   GARRY: **So!**

20   JULIE: **What do you mean, "so". You've already been**

21   **accepted to law school. You can't flunk now.**

22   GARRY: **I can if I want to.**

23   JULIE: **What's the matter with you? In all the time we've**

24   **been going together I've never seen you like this.**

25   GARRY: **Nothing's wrong with me. Maybe I just don't want**

26   **to be a lawyer anymore.**

27   JULIE: **Bull, you've wanted to be a lawyer as long as I've**

28   **known you. What do you think your parents would say?**

29   GARRY: **I don't care what my parents say.**

30   JULIE: **That came out a little hostile, didn't it?**

31   GARRY: *No it didn't!*

32   JULIE: **Excuse me.** *(Pause)* **Did you have a fight with your**

33   **parents?**

34   GARRY: **No, and don't bring up my damn parents anymore.**

35   JULIE: **Fine!** *(She packs up her books and starts to leave.)*

1   GARRY: Don't go. I'm sorry, come here, please. *(She comes a*
2   *little begrudgingly and sits on his lap.)* I didn't mean to yell
3   at you. Also, my parents have been getting to me.
4   JULIE: How?
5   GARRY: Well, everytime I talk to them, all they ever talk
6   about is law school. I'm not sure if I ever wanted to go
7   to law school.
8   JULIE: So instead of telling them, you flunk out and *bingo*,
9   no problem.
10   GARRY: Yeah, I guess so.
11   JULIE: Why don't you talk to them.?
12   GARRY: Cause, they're not like your folks. They let you be
13   what you want to be.
14   JULIE: Is there something else you want to be?
15   GARRY: Yeah, but they wouldn't understand.
16   JULIE: How do you know till you talk to them. *(Pause)* What
17   is it?
18   GARRY: *(Starts to talk)* Naa. Let's fool around.
19   JULIE: No. What is it?
20   GARRY: *(Pause)* A terrorist. *(They both start to laugh.)*
21   JULIE: No really, is there something that you want to do
22   you've never told anyone?
23   GARRY: That's just it. I'm not sure anymore. I'm twenty-one
24   and very confused.
25   JULIE: So, unconfuse yourself.
26   GARRY: How?
27   JULIE: *(Pause)* Let's play "Think Fast."
28   GARRY: Not at four in the morning!
29   JULIE: *(She starts squirting him.)* Come on, what do you want
30   to do right after graduation? Think fast.
31   GARRY: OK, I want to take you to Europe and see how many
32   countries we can have sex in.
33   JULIE: Tell that to your parents.
34   GARRY: Right. I've got a good picture of that.
35   JULIE: Just tell them we want to get away.

1   GARRY: What if they say no?
2   JULIE: So, you don't need their permission. You have your
3   own money. We'll just go, take all the time we need. Law
4   school will always be here.
5   GARRY: What if I decide I don't want law school.
6   JULIE: Then you'll do something else, but don't screw that
7   possibility by flunking this test.
8   GARRY: OK, back to the hyperola?
9   JULIE: Where's my gun?
10   GARRY: Why?
11   JULIE: Because it's hypotenuse.
12   GARRY: Julie?
13   JULIE: What?
14   GARRY: Nobody cares. *(He produces the gun and starts squirting*
15   *her.)*
16   **END**
17
18
19
20
21
22
23
24
25
26
27
28
29
30
31
32
33
34
35

My Home is Your Home

CAST: Joel — 20s; Kevin — 20s.

SCENE OPENS: Kevin is lying on the couch. There is a cloth over his eyes. Joel enters holding a shirt. He is standing behind the couch. He is very mad. He does not see Kevin.

JOEL: Kevin, Kevin, are you in here?

KEVIN: *(In pain)* Oh, God.

JOEL: Kevin, where are you?

KEVIN: If I answer will you go away?

JOEL: *(JOEL walks around to the front of the couch.)* Well, it's nice to see you up considering that it's two o'clock in the afternoon.

KEVIN: I'm not up. That's only a rumor.

JOEL: Funny! You care to explain this? *(JOEL sticks the shirt in KEVIN'S face. He does not see it since the cloth is still over his eyes.)*

KEVIN: What?

JOEL: This!

KEVIN: *(KEVIN sits up and takes the cloth off his eyes.)* It's a shirt. *(He lays back down and replaces the cloth.)*

JOEL: Is that all you have to say?

KEVIN: No, I think it's a very nice shirt.

JOEL: *(JOEL pulls the cloth off KEVIN'S eyes.)* I want to know why this shirt was in the freezer.

KEVIN: The refrigerator was full.

JOEL: All right, cut it out. What I really want to know is why I was awakened at two a.m. by you and your date, kept up for three hours and in the morning I find this in the freezer. What the hell were you doing?

KEVIN: Do you really want to know?

JOEL: Yes.

KEVIN: OK, I was playing a game. *(He sits up.)*

JOEL: What game?

1   KEVIN: I like to call it "Eskomos in the frozen Tundra."

2   JOEL: That's sick.

3   KEVIN: Only if you play it right.

4   JOEL: Enough of this. I want to talk to you.

5   KEVIN: OK, OK, stop yelling. Jesus, what's wrong with you.

6   You got a problem?

7   JOEL: Yes.

8   KEVIN: Well, what is it?

9   JOEL: *You!*

10   KEVIN: Me? What did I do?

11   JOEL: What haven't you done. You came to spend the

12   weekend with me five weeks ago. In that time you have

13   turned my apartment into a nuclear waste dump, you

14   have people here at all hours, and you're making me a

15   nervous wreck.

16   KEVIN: I'm not trying to make you nervous. I'm just trying

17   to get you to relax, to have a good time. Look Joel, you're

18   my brother and it hurts me to see you so uptight. I'm

19   trying to help you to have some fun.

20   JOEL: Fun, fun? The one night I agreed to go out on the

21   town with you it took me three days to recover.

22   KEVIN: But we did have fun.

23   JOEL: That's not my point. You don't know what I'm trying

24   to say, do you?

25   KEVIN: No. Why don't you just say it.

26   JOEL: OK. *(Pause)* You're right, we are brothers and because

27   we are I feel that I can tell you this from the bottom of

28   my heart.

29   KEVIN: What?

30   JOEL: *Get out!*

31   KEVIN: What?

32   JOEL: Pack up your slop and get out.

33   KEVIN: Why?

34   JOEL: Ever since we were kids you have always taken over

35   everything that was mine. You pushed me aside. Well, I

1   see it happening again and I'm going to stop it before it

2   continues.

3   KEVIN: When did I ever do that?

4   JOEL: How about that big date I had with Carrie Ruffo. I

5   got to her house and she had already gone out with you.

6   KEVIN: That was one date. Why are you making such a big

7   deal about it?

8   JOEL: Because it was my prom night.

9   KEVIN: Oh. *(Pause)* Well, maybe you were right about that.

10   JOEL: It's not just that one case. There were a lot of them.

11   Anytime I did anything on my own, you butted in and

12   took over.

13   KEVIN: You finished?

14   JOEL: I haven't really started yet. When we were kids you

15   were an egotistical, self-centered leech. I thought you

16   might grow out of it, but you're more of a leech than ever.

17   You don't want to work. You want to waltz through life.

18   Well, that's fine, but not in my apartment. Maybe if I kick

19   you out you'll learn some responsibility and stop being

20   a bum.

21   KEVIN: A bum? Oh, I see. You want me to grow up and be

22   just like you, a twenty-three-year-old middle aged,

23   wallflower wimp.

24   JOEL: Wimp? Is that what you think?

25   KEVIN: I just call 'em like I see them.

26   JOEL: Kevin, you've been asking for this for a long time. *(He

27   jumps at KEVIN. The two fall on the floor in an absurd struggle.)*

28   KEVIN: *(Yelling)* Wait, wait. You win. This isn't getting us

29   anywhere. *(They stop fighting.)* Jesus, you're really serious

30   about this, aren't you?

31   JOEL: Damn right.

32   KEVIN: Maybe you're right. I'll have to think about it.

33   JOEL: Don't think about it. *Do it!*

34   KEVIN: I will. You still want me to leave?

35   JOEL: I think it would be best.

1   KEVIN: You're right. All right, I'll pack up and go back to
2   L.A. I'll have to start being a responsible adult. No more
3   relying on others. Before I go, can I ask you a question.
4   JOEL: What?
5   KEVIN: Can I borrow your car and some money to get back?
6   *(Lights out.)*
7   **END**
8
9
10
11
12
13
14
15
16
17
18
19
20
21
22
23
24
25
26
27
28
29
30
31
32
33
34
35

The Blind Date

CAST: Jeff — age open; Karen — age open.

SCENE OPENS: Karen is setting up for an aerobics class. She is an aerobics instructor, and she looks the part. Enters, Jeff Michaels. He looks around, not at all sure what he's doing here.

KAREN: Can I help you?

JEFF: Hi. I'm not sure. Is this where the ten o'clock aerobics class is held?

KAREN: Yeah, but you're about a half hour early.

JEFF: I know, but I wanted to find out a little about these classes first.

KAREN: Why?

JEFF: Well, see, this may sound a little silly, but I have this date with an aerobics teacher tonight and I wanted to see what this stuff was all about.

KAREN: Have you taken an aerobics class before?

JEFF: No.

KAREN: Well, we do a lot of this. *(She turns on a tape and goes into a small routine. JEFF watches for a minute then turns to leave. KAREN turns off the tape.)* **Hey, where are you going?**

JEFF: To see if I can get a date with a librarian.

KAREN: I'm sorry. I didn't mean to scare you. Why don't we sit down and stretch before the class starts.

JEFF: That I know how to do. *(They both sit on the floor and start to do some stretching exercises.)*

KAREN: So, where does this girl teach aerobics?

JEFF: I don't know.

KAREN: Well, what kind of class does she teach?

JEFF: I don't know.

KAREN: *(She stops stretching for a minute.)* **What do you know?**

JEFF: Not much. See, it's a blind date that some friends of mine set up. I decided to take this class so at least we would have something to talk about.

1   KAREN: Can I ask you a question?

2   JEFF: Sure, what?

3   KAREN: Why do you need a blind date?

4   JEFF: Well, that's a little hard to explain.

5   KAREN: Oh, well, if you don't want to talk about it, that's

6   OK, I understand.

7   JEFF: No, it's fine. Actually, I feel a lot better when I do talk

8   about it.

9   KAREN: OK, so why do you need a blind date?

10   JEFF: See, I broke up with this girl three months ago and

11   it was very painful. I haven't wanted to go out with

12   anyone else since.

13   KAREN: *(She get's up and starts to help JEFF with his stretching.)*

14   I'm really sorry. How long were you going out with her?

15   JEFF: Two weeks.

16   KAREN: *(She stops.)* Let me get this straight. You've been

17   mourning the end of a relationship for three months that

18   lasted two weeks?

19   JEFF: Yup.

20   KAREN: If you don't mind my saying so, don't you think

21   that's a little out of proportion?

22   JEFF: That's what my friend Doug said, but he went a little

23   further and said that if I didn't get out soon, in another

24   week I'd be ready for a monastery.

25   KAREN: Was it this friend Doug who set up the date?

26   JEFF: Yeah, he said that I had no choice. If I didn't show up

27   he was going to bring this girl, Karen Miller, over to my

28   apartment. So I said I'd show up.

29   KAREN: You don't seem very excited about it.

30   JEFF: I'm not.

31   KAREN: Why?

32   JEFF: I don't like being pushed into situations.

33   KAREN: *(She sits next to him and they just talk.)* I know what

34   you mean. I've been on a few blind dates myself. If you

35   like each other, it's OK, but if you don't hit it off, it can

1   be a total disaster.

2   JEFF: Exactly, plus I'm not good in situations like this. I like

3   meeting people in my own way. I hate searching for

4   conversation when you don't know a person at all.

5   KAREN: So, this is why you're taking my class, to have

6   something to talk about?

7   JEFF: Yeah. Do you think it's a dumb idea?

8   KAREN: No, not at all. You're trying to learn about her

9   profession so you can talk to her about it. I think that's

10   very sweet.

11   JEFF: Thank you.

12   KAREN: Have you decided what you are going to do?

13   JEFF: Yeah. I'm going to suggest that we make love without

14   meaning.

15   KAREN: What?

16   JEFF: What's wrong, too forward? *(They both start to laugh.)*

17   No, we'll be going to dinner with my friend Doug and his

18   girlfriend.

19   KAREN: Sounds nice.

20   JEFF: Yeah. I'll tell you something. I hope she's as easy to

21   talk to as you are.

22   KAREN: Thanks. I'll tell you something. I think you'll do fine

23   tonight. You're very easy to talk to also. If I met you on

24   a blind date, I'd have no problem. Also, you don't need

25   to take a class to have something to talk about.

26   JEFF: Good. I have a feeling if I took your class, I'd be in no

27   shape for tonight. *(He get's up and starts to leave, then turns*

28   *back to her.)* If this doesn't work tonight, would you be

29   interested in having dinner some night?

30   KAREN: That would be very nice.

31   JEFF: By the way, my name's Jeff. Jeff Michaels. *(He holds*

32   *out his hand and goes back to her.)*

33   KAREN: My name's Karen.

34   JEFF: Karen?

35   KAREN: Yeah. Karen Miller. *(Pause)* Nice to meet you.

1	**JEFF:** *(JEFF laughs a little, realizing this is his date.)* **Hi, nice to**
2	**meet you, too.** *(They shake hands.)*
3	*(Lights out.)*
4	**END**
5	
6	
7	
8	
9	
10	
11	
12	
13	
14	
15	
16	
17	
18	
19	
20	
21	
22	
23	
24	
25	
26	
27	
28	
29	
30	
31	
32	
33	
34	
35	

Nice to Meet You

CAST: Sally — 20s; Jean — age open.

SCENE OPENS: Sally is seated in the living room of her house. She is in her twenties, pretty. She is married to a producer. Jean enters, unannounced. Sally is a little taken back as Jean just walks in. Jean is older than Sally and was married to Sally's husband.

SALLY: Excuse me, may I help you?

JEAN: No, I know the way. *(She starts across the room.)*

SALLY: Who are you?

JEAN: I'm not in the habit of introducing myself to the help.

SALLY: The help! All right, look lady, I don't know who you are but if you don't tell me how you got in here and what you want, I'm calling the cops and having you arrested for breaking into my house.

JEAN: Your house! You can't be Sally.

SALLY: Yes I can, and who the hell are you?

JEAN: Paul's description wasn't very good. Somehow, I pictured you *(Pause)* younger.

SALLY: *(Realizing)* Wait a minute, I know who you are. You're Paul's ex, right?

JEAN: How did you know?

SALLY: Paul said that you might be flying in on your broom some day.

JEAN: Did Paul call me a witch?

SALLY: Actually, he described you a different way.

JEAN: And how was that?

SALLY: Let's just say that it rhymes with witch.

JEAN: Charming as ever I see.

SALLY: Now that the introductions are over, what can I do for you?

JEAN: I'm here to pick up some of the things I left.

SALLY: Paul said that some of your stuff was still in the

– 52 –

1   storage shed.

2   JEAN: You mean he didn't burn them?

3   SALLY: Of course not.

4   JEAN: *(Sarcastically)* Decent of him.

5   SALLY: Look, why didn't you just say that you wanted your

6   stuff instead of barging in here like the "Bitch of the

7   Year?"

8   JEAN: I'm sorry. It hasn't been a great day and I always get

9   a little edgy and hostile when I come over here.

10   SALLY: Apology accepted. Would you care to sit down? *(She*

11   *sits.)* Now then, I'm Sally Peabody.

12   JEAN: I'm Jean Peabody. *(There's a nervous laugh between*

13   *them.)*

14   SALLY: Well what can I get for you?

15   JEAN: *(Confessing)* To be perfectly honest, nothing really.

16   When I heard that Paul had married, I had to check you

17   out.

18   SALLY: Why?

19   JEAN: I'm not sure. I guess I was interested in what way he

20   went.

21   SALLY: Do I pass inspection? *(They both laugh.)* As long as

22   we're being honest, let me ask you a question.

23   JEAN: All right.

24   SALLY: When you and Paul got divorced, why didn't you

25   keep the house?

26   JEAN: I wanted to make a clean break. I had a good job, we

27   split most of the property, but the house, *(Looks around)*

28   I didn't need it.

29   SALLY: Well, I'm glad about that.

30   JEAN: How did you and Paul meet?

31   SALLY: Working on his last film.

32   JEAN: You were one of the actresses or extras?

33   SALLY: No, I wrote the script.

34   JEAN: You're a writer?

35   SALLY: That's another way to put it.

1	JEAN:	Why did you decide to get married?
2	SALLY:	Why did you decide to get divorced?
3	JEAN:	Paul never told you?
4	SALLY:	Not really.
5	JEAN:	Let me answer by asking you a question.
6	SALLY:	OK.
7	JEAN:	What are some of Paul's habits?
8	SALLY:	Well, he always wears socks to bed.
9	JEAN:	Anything else?
10	SALLY:	He has a funny way of breathing at night and he has
11		to have his tirades at breakfast.
12	JEAN:	What do you think of them?
13	SALLY:	I don't know, they're kind of cute. They're part of him.
14	JEAN:	See, I never found them cute. As a matter of fact, after
15		nineteen years of marriage they drove me up the wall.
16	SALLY:	You divorced him because of his habits?
17	JEAN:	No, but they didn't help. We drifted apart. He never
18		took me seriously. We never talked. I was a part of his
19		world, but he was never a part of mine.
20	SALLY:	That's too bad. I think what's different with us is
21		when we met each other we each had our own worlds.
22		We became friends, learned about each other and merged
23		our lives.
24	JEAN:	That sounds nice.
25	SALLY:	It is.
26	JEAN:	Well, I wish you all the best. *(Pause)* I really do. You're
27		actually a nice person.
28	SALLY:	So are you and I really wanted to hate you too. *(They*
29		*both laugh.)*
30	JEAN:	I think it's time I left. It was nice to meet you.
31	SALLY:	Same here. *(JEAN starts to exit.)* **Jean?**
32	JEAN:	What?
33	SALLY:	Would you like to have lunch sometime?
34	JEAN:	That would be nice. I'll call you. *(They say goodby. She exits.)*
35		**END**

Eviction

CAST: Jenny — age open; Ted — age open.

SCENE OPENS: Jenny and Ted are on a sofa in an embrace.
   Suddenly Jenny breaks away. Jenny is about twenty-five, very
   pretty, intelligent, and self-assured. Ted is about the same age.
   He is a guy who likes fun, but very irresponsible.

JENNY: Enough of this. I'm leaving.

TED: Why?

**JENNY: Because I have a lot of things to do today. Isn't there
   something you have to do, like employment, for example.**

TED: Nope, not a thing.

JENNY: I was afraid of that. *(She finishes getting dressed, reaches
   into her purse, and pulls out a letter. She gives it to him.)* **Here,
   this is for you.**

TED: That's nice. You didn't have to get me a card.

JENNY: I didn't. Read it.

TED: *(He opens it and reads it. He gets a little shaken.)* **I don't
   believe it. Do you know what this is?**

JENNY: It's an eviction notice.

TED: No, it's an eviction notice.

**JENNY: You're being thrown out for not paying your rent
   for the last three months.**

**TED: I'm being thrown out for not paying rent for the last
   three months.** *(Pause)* **Wait a minute, how do you know
   all this? Do you do all the deliveries for this** *(Searching
   for the name)* **M. J. Kennedy?**

JENNY: No, I don't do deliveries. *(Pause)* **I am M. J. Kennedy.**

TED: What?

JENNY: Mary Jennifer Kennedy. I manage this building.

TED: I don't believe it!

JENNY: Start.

TED: Are you going to throw me out, just like that?

JENNY: It's hardly just like that. You haven't paid rent in

1   three months.

2   TED: But Jenny, how can you evict me, especially after what

3   we just did?

4   JENNY: Well, I certainly wouldn't have thrown you out

5   before.

6   TED: That's not funny.

7   JENNY: I'm not trying to be. Look Ted, I like you. I think

8   you're a nice guy and I like being with you, but business

9   is business. This is my job and I'm not going to let my

10   personal feelings interfere with that.

11   TED: What do you mean, your job?

12   JENNY: If you were listening, I said that I manage this

13   building.

14   TED: *(TED gets up and starts to dress.)* Well, no offense to you,

15   but I'm not going to take this.

16   JENNY: Oh really? What are you going to do?

17   TED: I'm going to find the guy who owns this building. We

18   are going to have it out. Where's this guy's office?

19   JENNY: Downtown, but you won't find him there. Daddy's

20   in Palm Springs for the week.

21   TED: Daddy? *(He sits down.)*

22   JENNY: I'll explain. I graduated college with a masters in

23   business and no job. I approached my father who owns

24   several buildings in the area and asked if I could manage one.

25   TED: Oh, I see. He's doing you a favor.

26   JENNY: Bull! I work my butt off here. You can check the

27   books or anything you want. This place is impeccably

28   run. Just because the owner is my father doesn't mean

29   that I get treated differently from any other manager. In

30   fact, I usually get scrutinized more.

31   TED: OK, OK, you're a terrific building manager. I believe

32   you, but can't you cut me a break?

33   JENNY: I've been cutting you a break. I can't carry you

34   anymore.

35   TED: Well, how about if I move in with you?

1   JENNY: *(Laughing)* **You're kidding, right?**

2   TED: **No.**

3   JENNY: **No, you can't move in with me. Stop looking for the**

4   **easy way out.**

5   TED: **I'm not looking . . .**

6   JENNY: *(Cutting him off)* **Yes you are. As far as I know, you**

7   **don't work, you have no visible means of support and**

8   **now you want me to support you. Forget it!**

9   TED: **That's not true.**

10   JENNY: **Then tell what's true.**

11   TED: **I don't know, but I do know that I'm trying. A writer**

12   **doesn't make it overnight. Also, you have no idea what**

13   **I've written and how hard I'm pushing. I do a hell of a**

14   **lot of work, I just don't get paid for it yet.**

15   JENNY: **Then you better start living within your means till**

16   **you sell something. You're hardly the only one with a**

17   **struggling career, you know. Grow up.**

18   TED: **Isn't there anything you can do for me?**

19   JENNY: *(Thinking)* **OK, I'll do this. You've got till the end of**

20   **the week to get the money you owe, *plus* one month in**

21   **advance. If you can do that, I'll let you stay. If not, you go.**

22   TED: *(Resigned)* **Thanks. I guess that's all I can ask you to do.**

23   JENNY: **It is.** *(She starts to leave.)*

24   TED: **Jenny, can I see you again?**

25   JENNY: **That's up to you. I'll let you know at the end of the**

26   **week.**

27   TED: **What happens then?**

28   JENNY: **We'll see if you're serious about trying. I can't afford**

29   **to invest my time in a con artist.**

30   TED: **I'm serious.**

31   JENNY: *(She walks over and gives him a kiss.)* **I hope so.** *(She*

32   *exits.)*

33   *(Lights out.)*

34   **END**

35

The Coach

CAST: Peter — 18; P.J. — 15 or 16.

SCENE OPENS: Peter is on the phone, trying to get a date. Peter is about eighteen-years-old. P.J. enters the room. P.J. is Peter's younger brother. He is about fifteen.

PETER: Yeah, so Betty, I was thinking that maybe, you know, if you're not busy . . .

P.J.   *(P.J. walks in and interrupts.)* **Peter, do you think I can borrow your black shirt?**

PETER: *(PETER covers the phone.)* **Would you wait a minute. I'm on the phone.** *(P.J. sits and watches PETER on the phone.)* **So anyway Betty, I was thinking that if you're not busy on Friday, maybe we could, you know, go to the movies or something.** *(Pause)* **Oh, how about Saturday?** *(Pause)* **Sunday?** *(Pause)* **1991? Hello. Hello?** *(He hangs up the phone.)*

P.J.   **Facing another exciting Friday night, huh?**

PETER: **Stick it.**

P.J.   **Good come back.**

PETER: **Look, I don't have time for you now. I have a lot of problems.**

P.J.   **I can tell from your phone call.**

PETER: **I don't need criticism from a pre-pubescent little twit who . . .**

P.J.   *(Cutting him off)* **Has a date Friday night.**

PETER: **Well, who cares. Anybody can get a date with a fifteen-year-old.**

P.J.   **True, but not just anybody can get a date with Margie Cutler.**

PETER: *(This stops PETER in his tracks.)* **Margie Cutler? My Margie Cutler? You have a date with Margie Cutler?**

P.J.   **Yeah, and what do you mean, "my Margie Cutler?"**

PETER: **Margie Cutler, the girl who sits next to me in geometry. I asked her out two months ago.**

1   P.J.   And one hour ago.

2   PETER: How did you know?

3   P.J.   She just called me up, *(Pause)* laughing.

4   PETER: Great.

5   P.J.   Don't get discouraged. I think I can get you a date with
6   her sister.

7   PETER: She's fifteen.

8   P.J.   Well, she likes older men.

9   PETER: Terrific. *(PETER sits.)*

10   P.J.   Look Peter, let's talk.

11   PETER: P.J., what the hell are we going to talk about?

12   P.J.   Your approach, for one thing.

13   PETER: What's wrong with my approach?

14   P.J.   It stinks.

15   PETER: What do you mean it stinks. How do you know?

16   P.J.   Margie Cutler told me.

17   PETER: What did she say?

18   P.J.   Well, she said . . .

19   PETER: *(Cutting him off)* Never mind. I know what she said.
20   What am I doing wrong?

21   P.J.   *(P.J. gets up and walks to the mirror.)* Come here. *(Pause)*
22   Come here. Look at yourself. You're a good looking guy.
23   You dress fine, thanks to me. The problem is you have
24   the personality of Norman Nerd.

25   PETER: Wait a minute. I've been told that I'm very sexy.

26   P.J.   Mom doesn't count.

27   PETER: What do you suggest I do?

28   P.J.   Let me show you how I see you. *(He picks up the phone*
29   *and ad libs a conversation.)* Betty, hi. You don't want to go
30   out with me Friday, do you. I didn't think so. Bye.

31   PETER: Again, what do you suggest?

32   P.J.   Don't give them a choice, give them details.

33   PETER: What?

34   P.J.   Tell them you're going out. Tell them what to wear, what
35   to bring, when to be ready, but don't ask.

1	PETER:	What if they say no?
2	P.J.	I don't know, they never have. Look, I've been dating
3		since I was ten. I know what I'm talking about.
4	PETER:	P.J., this is very tough for me. Here I am, the older
5		brother and I'm getting advice on women from my little
6		brother.
7	P.J.	Does it really matter?
8	PETER:	But I'm the one who's supposed to be more
9		experienced. I'm supposed to give the advice.
10	P.J.	Where is it written, Peter? You happen to be a really
11		great guy who's shy and insecure. If you act a little more
12		like me when you're with girls, you'll have no problem.
13	PETER:	But I don't like rejection.
14	P.J.	Who does?
15	PETER:	Hold on, it goes deeper than that. I'm so afraid of
16		being rejected or laughed at that I just don't go out. It's
17		much safer that way.
18	P.J.	That's very true, but I don't think you want to go through
19		your life safe and alone. Extend yourself. Take a chance.
20	PETER:	So, what do I do?
21	P.J.	Take the lead. Call up Betty and tell her you're going
22		out Friday.
23	PETER:	But ...
24	P.J.	But nothing. Do it!
25	PETER:	What do I say?
26	P.J.	Say, "Betty, Pete. Friday night, we're going out. I'll pick
27		you up at seven-thirty. Any questions? Good." That's it.
28	PETER:	I don't know. *(P.J. picks up the phone and dials. He*
29		*hands the phone to PETER.)* Betty, Pete. Friday night, we're
30		going out. I'll pick you up at seven-thirty. Any questions?
31		Good. *(He hangs up.)*
32	P.J.	All right.
33	PETER:	Thanks. By the way, how do you know all this?
34	P.J.	I read a lot.
35	PETER:	Oh. Is that all?

```
1    P.J.   No.
2    PETER:   What else?
3    P.J.   I think big.
4                          END
5
6
7
8
9
10
11
12
13
14
15
16
17
18
19
20
21
22
23
24
25
26
27
28
29
30
31
32
33
34
35
```

The Mixer

CAST: Bobby — college age; Jack — college age.

SCENE OPENS: We are in a dorm room in any college. Bobby and Jack are roommates. At present Jack is fixing himself up to go out. Bobby is reading. He is supposed to be going with Jack.

JACK: **Bobby, come on, shake a leg. The party is starting in less than an hour.**

BOBBY: *(BOBBY sitting in his chair then shakes his leg without ever looking up from his book.)* **Is that enough, or should I shake it a little more?**

JACK: **Oh God, you're in one of those moods.**

BOBBY: *(BOBBY then lowers the book.)* **Jack, would you answer me a question?**

JACK: **What?**

BOBBY: **How does gyrating ones appendage hasten the process at which one gets dressed.**

JACK: **OK, professor, never mind. Just get ready. The girls will be here soon.**

BOBBY: **No.** *(He starts reading again.)*

JACK: **What do you mean, "No?"**

BOBBY: **"No: the negative response. Not in the affirmative…"**

JACK: *(Cutting him off)* **Enough, I know what no means.**

BOBBY: **Good.**

JACK: **But why?**

BOBBY: **Why, what?**

JACK: **Why aren't you getting dressed for the mixer.**

BOBBY: **Oh, that's easy. I'm not getting dressed because I'm not going.**

JACK: **Oh yes you are! You're not pulling this crap on me again.**

BOBBY: **What crap?**

JACK: **What you always do. I bust my butt getting you a date,**

1   then you cop out right before it's time to go out.

2   BOBBY: When did I ever do that?

3   JACK: You want to start with this year, or should I start

4   when we were freshman.

5   BOBBY: Never mind. OK, I've done it a couple of times.

6   JACK: A couple? You've done this everytime Stacy and I set

7   you up.

8   BOBBY: Maybe that should tell you something.

9   JACK: What?

10   BOBBY: *Stop setting me up.* Now, if you don't mind, Plato

11   and I have a date for the evening. *(He goes back to reading.*

12   *JACK takes his book away.)*

13   JACK: Forget that, you're coming with us tonight. You'll

14   really like Sharon. She's great.

15   BOBBY: I'm sure she is. All the girls you and Stacy have set

16   me up with have been great.

17   JACK: Then what's the problem.

18   BOBBY: I hate mixers!

19   JACK: I've known it, but you never told me that.

20   BOBBY: I've always told you that. You just never listen. How

21   many mixers have we gone to since we've been in college?

22   JACK: I don't know.

23   BOBBY: Take a guess.

24   JACK: Fifty.

25   BOBBY: Close, fifty-three. And how many have I stayed

26   longer than an hour.

27   JACK: I don't know.

28   BOBBY: One, and I only stayed longer at that one because

29   I got locked in the bathroom and nobody noticed for three

30   hours.

31   JACK: All right, you don't like mixers. I'll concede to you on

32   that counselor. But do me a favor and go to this one.

33   BOBBY: No.

34   JACK: Come on, I promise it won't be like the last fifty-three

35   times.

1	BOBBY:	How do you know that?

1   BOBBY: How do you know that?
2   JACK: Cause I won't let it. I know that you don't like mixers,
3   but you've only got yourself to blame for most of the bad
4   times at them.
5   BOBBY: And how did you arrive at that?
6   JACK: Because I've seen you at them. This is how you look.
7   *(He stands in a corner, not looking at anyone, just staring down*
8   *and shuffling his feet.)*
9   BOBBY: I do not.
10   JACK: Yes you do. Hey, if I can prove it, will you go?
11   BOBBY: *(Laughing)* Sure, but you can't prove it.
12   JACK: Wait here. *(He goes to the shelf and gets a yearbook. He*
13   *sits next to BOBBY and opens the book, looks for, and finds the*
14   *right page.)*
15   BOBBY: What's this?
16   JACK: It's the yearbook from last year. This picture is from
17   the homecoming dance. Take a look in the background.
18   See the guy in the corner in the back.
19   BOBBY: Yes.
20   JACK: I rest my case.
21   BOBBY: *(BOBBY takes the book out of JACK'S hands.)* That's
22   not . . . Yes it is. So what? This is one case.
23   JACK: You want me to show you some other pictures?
24   BOBBY: No, I'll concede this point to *you* counselor.
25   JACK: Thank you. Well, now that I've proven it, get dressed.
26   BOBBY: Jack, please don't make me go.
27   JACK: Look Bobby, you are a really great guy. Stacy and I
28   both agree. We're trying to figure out why you're alone.
29   Now I know. You just don't try. You like being in that
30   corner.
31   BOBBY: I don't like being there, it's just where I wind up. I
32   don't meet people very well, like you do. I'd love to have
33   the kind of girlfriend that you have. But I know I won't
34   meet her at a mixer.
35   JACK: How do you know till you give it a good try, and not

1   in a corner.
2 BOBBY: I'll make a deal with you. I'll go and give it an hour.
3   If I don't like it we leave. And I will try.
4 JACK: Make it two hours.
5 BOBBY: One and a half.
6 JACK: Deal. Now, shake a leg or we'll be late. *(BOBBY stands,*
7   *holds his leg out and shakes it.)*
8   *(Black out)*
9   **END**
10
11
12
13
14
15
16
17
18
19
20
21
22
23
24
25
26
27
28
29
30
31
32
33
34
35

Dinner Guest

CAST: Maggie — 20s; Tim — 20s.

SCENE OPENS: Maggie is in her apartment waiting for her boyfriend, Tim. She is straightening up. She is preparing for dinner. There is a knock on the door.

TIM: *(Offstage)* **Maggie honey, it's me. Open up.** *(MAGGIE goes to the door and lets TIM in. He gives her a kiss.)* **Hi, honey. I'm sorry I'm late, but I almost forgot the wine you wanted.**

MAGGIE: Hi, that's OK. Let me put the wine in the refrigerator. *(She exits.)*

TIM: *(TIM takes off his coat and looks at the table setting. He yells to MAGGIE in the kitchen.)* **Maggie, there are three places set for dinner. Who else is coming?**

MAGGIE: *(Offstage)* **I can't hear you.**

TIM: I said, there are three places set, who else is coming to dinner?

MAGGIE: *(MAGGIE enters from the kitchen.)* **I'm sorry honey, I couldn't hear you in the kitchen. Here, I made you a drink.**

TIM: You didn't answer my question.

MAGGIE: What question?

TIM: Who's coming to dinner?

MAGGIE: You look tired, sweetie. Why don't you go in the den with your drink and watch TV till dinner's ready.

TIM: OK, you're avoiding the question. I have a feeling I'm not going to like the answer.

MAGGIE: I don't know what you're talking about. *(Pause)* **Would you like me to massage you back.**

TIM: You want to massage my back?

MAGGIE: If you'd like.

TIM: Now I *know* I'm going to *hate* the answer. Who's coming to dinner?

MAGGIE: Well . . .

1   TIM: Wait a minute, you made me a drink, you want me to
2   relax, and you want to give me a massage. *(Pause)* **Oh no,**
3   your mother's coming, right?
4   MAGGIE: Well ...
5   TIM: I knew it. Have a nice dinner. Bye. *(He starts to leave.*
6   *MAGGIE blocks the door.)*
7   MAGGIE: Tim, don't leave. I really want all of us to have a
8   good dinner.
9   TIM: You really want this to be a good dinner?
10   MAGGIE: More than anything?
11   TIM: Then tell *dragon lady* to stay home.
12   MAGGIE: Thank you very much. I want you to know that I
13   have worked my butt off for this dinner and you're not
14   going to ruin it.
15   TIM: Hold on. Don't turn this around on me. It's not my fault
16   we don't get along.
17   MAGGIE: Well, that's why I want to have this dinner, so we
18   can straighten out this problem.
19   TIM: Forget it. You can't talk with a ... thing like that.
20   MAGGIE: That *thing* happens to be a person and that person
21   happens to be my mother.
22   TIM: Well, I'd like to see some proof of that.
23   MAGGIE: What, that she's my mother?
24   TIM: No, that she's really a person. I have this theory that
25   she was left in the woods when she was a baby and raised
26   by a nest of cobras as one of their own. *(Pause)* You know,
27   she carries the family line well.
28   MAGGIE: You know, it's not all her fault that you two got
29   off on the wrong foot. You had something to do with it, too.
30   TIM: Me? What did I do?
31   MAGGIE: You insulted her the first time you talked to her.
32   TIM: *What!* What? All I said the first time was, "Hi, Mrs.
33   Krane. It's nice to meet you." Then your mother said, "sit
34   on it, you scum sucking twerp." You want to explain how
35   I was to blame?

1   MAGGIE: OK, OK, so it wasn't your fault, but would you
2   please try and make an effort to help rectify the situation?
3   TIM: How?
4   MAGGIE: Apologize to my mother for your last meeting.
5   TIM: Are you kidding?
6   MAGGIE: Does that mean you won't do it?
7   TIM: Bingo
8   MAGGIE: You won't even try?
9   TIM: No. As a matter of fact, I don't think I'm going to stay.
10 MAGGIE: Fine. Leave then.
11 TIM: I will. *(He gets his coat and starts to leave. MAGGIE starts*
12   *to cry.)* Come on, don't cry like that.
13 MAGGIE: I'm sorry, it's the only way I know how to cry.
14 TIM: OK, let's sit down and talk. *(They both sit.)* This is really
15   very important to you isn't it?
16 MAGGIE: Yes. You want to know the reason my mother
17   didn't like you the first time you met?
18 TIM: You mean you know and you never told me?
19 MAGGIE: Yes. I didn't tell you cause I thought I could work
20   it out with my mother, but I couldn't.
21 TIM: Tell me.
22 MAGGIE: OK, do you remember when we broke up a little
23   while ago.
24 TIM: No, of course not. It was only the worst month of my
25   entire life.
26 MAGGIE: Mine too. See, when we were going through that,
27   you had never met my mother. She consoled me. Only
28   thing was, I never told her that the break-up had been a
29   mutual decision of ours. So she blamed you for my
30   unhappiness.
31 TIM: I can understand most of . . .
32 MAGGIE: Hold on, let me finish. See, my Dad died when I
33   was young and my mother has been very protective of
34   me, and in very loud ways. You've seen that. It upsets
35   her a lot when I'm upset. When we got back together, she

1   just didn't trust you. We've had a lot of fights about it.

2 TIM: So now you've decided for force the issue.

3 MAGGIE: I guess so. Timmy, I love you so much and I want

4   you and my mother to get along. For me, would you please

5   make an effort to patch things up. I know when she gets

6   to know you she'll love you as much as I do.

7 TIM: Because I love you too, *(Pause)* I'll try. We'll have dinner

8   and talk. *(MAGGIE gives him a hug.)* Don't expect too much,

9   though.

10 MAGGIE: OK. So, when mother comes in you'll give her a

11   hug and a kiss?

12 TIM: Don't push it. *(They both start to laugh.)*

13   **END**

14

15

16

17

18

19

20

21

22

23

24

25

26

27

28

29

30

31

32

33

34

35

The Stakeout

CAST: Ron — 20s; Scott — 20s.

SCENE OPENS: Scott is standing in front of a mirror. He is a cop. He is dressing to go out on a stakeout. Offstage is his partner Ron. He is also preparing to go out with Scott on the stakeout. They are yelling at each other.

RON: *(Offstage)* **Scott!**

SCOTT: **What?**

RON: *(Offstage)* **Forget it. I'm not going through with this.**

SCOTT: **You don't have any choice.**

RON: *(Offstage)* **Wanna bet?**

SCOTT: **Would you stop complaining and get out here.**

RON: *No!*

SCOTT: *Now! (RON enters. He is dressed as a woman, not an attractive one, but a woman. SCOTT finds it hard to stifle his laughter.)* **You look . . . beautiful.** *(He starts to laugh hard.)*

RON: **That does it. I'm changing.** *(He starts to take the wig off.)*

SCOTT: **No, no. I'm sorry. It's just that I wasn't expecting . . . this.**

RON: **What did you think I was going to look like, Brooke Shields.?**

SCOTT: **No, I wasn't expecting Brooke Shields, but I wasn't expecting Tug Boat Annie either.** *(SCOTT starts to laugh again. RON rips the wig off and throws it on the floor.)*

RON: **You think it's so funny, you wear the dress.**

SCOTT: **Come on, put the wig back on. We've got to get to the park.**

RON: **Scott, why do we have to do this?**

SCOTT: **Because in this precinct all the detectives take turns at mugger patrol.**

RON: **Well, they didn't do this at my old precinct.**

SCOTT: **Well, you wanted to be transferred to where there was more action.**

1   RON: Yeah, but I always assumed I'd get to wear pants.
2   SCOTT: Welcome to Manhattan South.
3   RON: Great. So, what's the routine.
4   SCOTT: Nothing too tough. We wait till dark and just walk
5   around the park and wait to be mugged. If anyone goes
6   after me, you or the purse, we get him. There's been a lot
7   of problems by the lake lately. That's where we'll hang
8   out.
9   RON: OK, sounds good.
10   SCOTT: I just hope to God, nobody I know sees me with you.
11   RON: Why?
12   SCOTT: I've got a reputation around town of going out with
13   good looking ladies. You could blow that all to hell.
14   RON: You know, you're not exactly my idea of the ideal date
15   either. My girlfriend looked at me real strange when I
16   asked if I could borrow some eye make-up.
17   SCOTT: Speaking of that, you used too much eye liner.
18   RON: Who are you, Max Factor?
19   SCOTT: Fine don't listen to me. It's your business if you want
20   to go out looking like a cheap whore.
21   RON: I thought that was the idea, to look like a cheap whore.
22   SCOTT: That's *hooker patrol* not *mugger patrol*.
23   RON: Great, now I have to go re-do my eyes.
24   SCOTT: I'm kidding, they look fine, but that dress is way out
25   of style.
26   RON: *(Getting annoyed)* Would you stop. I'm nervous about
27   this.
28   SCOTT: Why?
29   RON: Never mind, you don't want to hear this.
30   SCOTT: Yeah, I do.
31   RON: OK, ever since I was a kid I wanted to be a cop. Then,
32   when I became a cop out on Long Island I realized that
33   I needed to be a cop here, where I could really do
34   something, so I transferred. Now what am I doing?
35   Playing a woman and hoping I get mugged. I want to do

1   well, so I don't have to be on mugger patrol forever.
2   SCOTT: Let me explain something to you. Everybody here
3   does this. We work as a team here. Nobody particularly
4   likes this work, but it is essential, so everyone takes their
5   turn.
6   RON: I know that, but I want to get into Vice or Homicide.
7   How long does that take?
8   SCOTT: Slow down. When you work in Manhattan you have
9   to walk before you run. This is probably the toughest city
10   for vice, homicide, and burglary cops. You just don't walk
11   in here and take over those jobs. It takes a little time to
12   see if you can cut it or if you *want* to cut it.
13   RON: How long does that take?
14   SCOTT: Depends on the man. There is no set formula. The
15   captain can usually tell. He's a good man. Want to know
16   a secret?
17   RON: What?
18   SCOTT: When you came here the captain showed me your
19   file and asked if I would partner with you. You had a
20   pretty impressive record. That burglary ring you broke
21   on the Island was good police work.
22   RON: Thanks.
23   SCOTT: Trust me, that scored points with the captain.
24   RON: Really?
25   SCOTT: Why would I lie? Anyway, I don't think it'll be too
26   long before you're doing the work you want. Just be
27   patient.
28   RON: OK. Thanks for the advice.
29   SCOTT: No charge.
30   RON: *(RON puts his wig on, then a jacket.)* **Well, I'm as ready as**
31   **I'll ever be. You ready?**
32   SCOTT: Yeah.
33   RON: Scott?
34   SCOTT: What?
35   RON: This is the first date. I hope you don't expect anything

1   when you bring me home.
2 SCOTT: Don't worry, any woman who wears *those* shoes with
3   *that* skirt, isn't worth the effort.
4 RON: What's wrong with these?
5   *(Lights out)*
6   **END**
7
8
9
10
11
12
13
14
15
16
17
18
19
20
21
22
23
24
25
26
27
28
29
30
31
32
33
34
35

PART 2:
DRAMA SCENES

The Story

CAST: Tracy — 20s— Vivian — age open.

SCENE OPENS: Tracy Gallagher is sitting in a dressing room.
She is a reporter for a not too respectable magazine. She is
waiting for Vivian Carter. Vivian is a producer, actress, a very
powerful lady. Vivian enters and notices Tracy sitting there.

VIVIAN: How did you get in here?

TRACY: I'm persistent.

VIVIAN: You're a pain.

TRACY: I'm a reporter.

VIVIAN: Is that what you call it?

TRACY: What's that supposed to mean?

VIVIAN: I didn't know that rag you work for hired reporters.
I thought they got their staff from under a rock.

TRACY: That's not fair. We print a lot of true stories.

VIVIAN: That's a laugh. You wouldn't know the truth if it
came up and bit you on the butt.

TRACY: That's not true.

VIVIAN: Oh really? How many times has that garbage can
you write for been sued for libel?

TRACY: (Pause) Oh, a couple.

VIVIAN: Today?

TRACY: All right, that may be, but I never have been. I'm an
honest reporter who goes after good stories.

VIVIAN: Ah, then you must be the one who wrote that story
called, "I Interviewed a Nympho From Neptune."

TRACY: (Pause) Why are you such a witch? What happened
to you?

VIVIAN: Wait a minute. I'm going to set the record straight
on that. Nothing's happened to me. I've always been this
way. I was a witch when I started out and now that I am
a very powerful actress and producer, I'm still a witch.

TRACY: Why?

1 VIVIAN: I believe in being consistent.
2 TRACY: Well, I have to admire your honesty.
3 VIVIAN: You should admire more than that. Now, if you don't
4   mind *get out,* before I call security!
5 TRACY: Just like that? The interview's over?
6 VIVIAN: Just like that and there was no interview.
7 TRACY: Why?
8 VIVIAN: I don't do interviews with pushy reporters.
9 TRACY: Who are you kidding? You don't do interviews at all.
10 VIVIAN: Very good. Maybe you're not as stupid as you look.
11 TRACY: Stick it. *(She gets up to leave, stops and turns.)* You know,
12   I've tried to be a good reporter. I've gone through all the
13   proper channels and the nicest thing your office said was,
14   "Buzz off!"
15 VIVIAN: They're under orders.
16 TRACY: That's what I figured. That's why I sneaked in here.
17   I wanted to be the first in a long time to interview you.
18   I've uncovered some facts that I wanted to discuss with
19   you.
20 VIVIAN: I couldn't care less what you've uncovered. Now,
21   get out!
22 TRACY: Fine. *(Pause)* Now I know why some reporters print
23   stories without talking to celebrities.
24 VIVIAN: And why's that?
25 TRACY: Because a lot of them act like you're acting now.
26   I'm going to write my story and I don't care if you sue
27   me. *(She starts to leave.)* Say hello to Jason for me.
28 VIVIAN: What do you know about Jason?
29 TRACY: Not much, except that he exists. That's why I wanted
30   to talk to you before I told the entire world that you had
31   a ten-year-old son. *(VIVIAN grabs her before she has a chance*
32   *to exit.)*
33 VIVIAN: You wouldn't dare?
34 TRACY: You know, you have a reputation for walking all
35   over people. Well I think it's about time somebody took a

1   stroll over you, and I think that it's going to be me.
2   VIVIAN: OK, I'll make a deal with you. I'll tell you about
3   Jason, but you can't print it.
4   TRACY: That's no deal, forget it.
5   VIVIAN: Please.
6   TRACY: Look, you be straight with me, tell me the story and
7   I'll decide. If not I'll just print what I know.
8   VIVIAN: I guess I have no choice, do I?
9   TRACY: No.
10   VIVIAN: Fine. *(They go back to sit. TRACY takes out her pad and*
11   *starts to write.)*
12   TRACY: Tell me about Jason.
13   VIVIAN: The story starts about fifteen years ago. I met and
14   married a man named Irv Glasser. After trying for five
15   years, I finally got pregnant and gave birth to Jason. That
16   was the time it was reported that I was going to retire.
17   Anyway, shortly after that my husband was killed by a
18   drunk driver. That's when I decided to shelter Jason from
19   this business. I didn't want him bothered.
20   TRACY: That's it? You didn't want him bothered. That's the
21   same thing all the stars say about their kids. I've heard
22   this a million times.
23   VIVIAN: Are you going to write about him?
24   TRACY: I see no reason not to.
25   VIVIAN: How about the fact that he's never had a normal
26   childhood?
27   TRACY: Why, because your a big shot actress?
28   VIVIAN: No.
29   TRACY: Because you're a big producer?
30   VIVIAN: No.
31   TRACY: Then why?
32   VIVIAN: *(VIVIAN gets up and starts to yell.)* **Because he's**
33   **austistic!** *(Silence.)*
34   TRACY: What?
35   VIVIAN: What word didn't you understand?

1	TRACY: Why didn't you just say so?
2	VIVIAN: Frankly, it's none of your business. When Irv and
3	I found out we didn't want the press to find out. We
4	wanted our privacy. Then when Irv died I sheltered
5	Jason. I spent all my free time with him. I didn't want
6	him bothered by people or a world he could never *possibly*
7	understand, and that's the way I want to keep it.
8	**TRACY:** *(TRACY rips out the pages from her pad. Rips them up*
9	*and hands them to VIVIAN.)* **Then that's the way it'll be.**
10	VIVIAN: Thank you. *(TRACY gets up and starts to leave.)* Excuse
11	me.
12	TRACY: What?
13	VIVIAN: Before you go, would you like to know how the new
14	movie's going?
15	TRACY: *(TRACY sits down and takes out her pad.)* Shoot.
16	END
17	
18	
19	
20	
21	
22	
23	
24	
25	
26	
27	
28	
29	
30	
31	
32	
33	
34	
35	

The Break-Up

CAST: Mickey — age open; J.J. — age open.

SCENE OPENS: We are in a restaurant. J.J. is seated at a table. She is waiting for her boyfriend, Mickey, to show up. Obviously by her actions, she is annoyed.

MICKEY: Hi, honey. I'm sorry I'm late, but I was in the middle of a meeting and I couldn't get away. (He gives her a kiss and sits down.)

J.J.   Well, you could have called. I've been waiting for forty-five minutes.

MICKEY: I said I was sorry. Now, what's up?

J.J.   I think it's time we had a serious talk.

MICKEY: About what?

J.J.   About us.

MICKEY: Oh, I see what this is all about. Look, I know I haven't been very attentive since I got a promotion. I'm sorry about that.

J.J.   That's partially it, but not all.

MICKEY: Then what's the problem?

J.J.   I'm not sure how to put this.

MICKEY: Then why don't you just say it straight out.

J.J.   I want a divorce.

MICKEY: What?

J.J.   I want a divorce. Don't you know what that means?

MICKEY: Of course I do, but I don't think we can get a divorce.

J.J.   Why not?

MICKEY: We're not married.

J.J.   I know that, but I wasn't speaking literally. What I mean is that we should stop seeing each other. We have a lot of problems.

MICKEY: I'm confused. Up to three minutes ago I didn't know we had any problems.

1   J.J.   Well, maybe if you had listened to me you would have.

2   MICKEY: When did you ever say anything was wrong?

3   J.J.   Right before you left on your trip.

4   MICKEY: What? When . . . *(Pause)* Oh come on. If I remember
5   correctly I had a cab honking downstairs, an eight a.m.
6   flight to catch, and you on the phone saying, "When you
7   get back I want to talk to you about something." That
8   hardly sounded like an emergency to me.

9   J.J.   Maybe if you had read in between the lines you would
10   have known it was.

11   MICKEY: Don't hand me that. We've never had any problems
12   talking before.

13   J.J.   That's beside the point. Anyway, it's in the open now,
14   and I want out of this relationship.

15   MICKEY: After a year and a half you just decided this?

16   J.J.   No, I've been thinking about this for months.

17   MICKEY: For months. I see. Instead of talking to me about
18   what's bothering you when it happens, you just let it
19   build up till you can't really decide what's an important
20   problem or not. Then to take the easy way out, you bring
21   me to a restaurant, where I won't make a scene, and just
22   drop this in my lap.

23   J.J.   Mickey, that's not fair.

24   MICKEY: You've got a lot of nerve talking about being fair.
25   You'll excuse me if I don't stay for the dessert. *(He starts*
26   *to rise.)*

27   J.J.   Where are you going?

28   MICKEY: Back to work.

29   J.J.   You're not going anywhere till you finish this discussion
30   you started.

31   MICKEY: I started?

32   J.J.   Fine, I started it. But now that it's in the open, I want
33   to finish it.

34   MICKEY: Then finish it. *(He sits back down.)*

35   J.J.   I want you to know something. My doubts about our

1	relationship weren't caused by you or me. They were
2	caused by us. It's our relationship. I started to feel like
3	I was choking. It's never been a question of whether I
4	love you or not. I do. I just don't know whether I love
5	you enough.
6	MICKEY: Thank you for telling me now. Do you think that
7	makes you special? You seem to think that you're the
8	only one with these feelings. I've been in the same
9	relationship and at times I felt strangled myself. There
10	were times I wanted out myself, but what I've always
11	known is that I love you more than anybody I've ever
12	loved. Also, I've always known that if we had a problem,
13	we could discuss it. Maybe I was wrong.
14	J.J. No you weren't. It's just that we started going out so
15	young. There are a lot of things I want to do on my own.
16	MICKEY: I never stopped you when you wanted to be alone.
17	J.J. I know, but I still feel like I belong to you. I don't want
18	to belong to anyone at this point.
19	MICKEY: Well, I belonged to you.
20	J.J. You wanted too, that's different.
21	MICKEY: Well, I guess there's not a whole lot more to say.
22	It's amazing how you can just dismiss the last eighteen
23	months like that.
24	J.J. You think that's how it is?
25	MICKEY: That's the way it looks.
26	J.J. Well, you're wrong. This is the hardest thing I've ever
27	had to do.
28	MICKEY: You seem to be doing it well.
29	J.J. There's no need for sarcasm, Mickey.
30	MICKEY: I'm not being sarcastic. If you want your freedom,
31	you've got it. Enjoy yourself.
32	J.J. Can we still be friends?
33	MICKEY: I don't know. None of my friends have ever hurt
34	me like this. I don't know if I can look at you as just "my
35	friend." So you'd better think about this long and hard

1   because if you think I'm going to wait around while you
2   learn about yourself, you're wrong.
3 J.J. If things don't work out, you think there might be a
4   chance of us getting back together.
5 MICKEY: I don't know if I'd put myself back into a place
6   where I'd let you hurt me again. So, I really don't know.
7 J.J. Do you still love me?
8 MICKEY: I'll always love you. I must admit that I don't like
9   you very much at this moment, but I still love you. Now
10   if there's nothing else, I'd like to leave.
11 J.J. You never answered me. What about us?
12 MICKEY: I guess we'll have to wait and see. Enjoy your
13   lunch. *(He exits.)*
14   **END**
15
16
17
18
19
20
21
22
23
24
25
26
27
28
29
30
31
32
33
34
35

Brotherhood

CAST: Joey — early 20s; Frank — early 20s.

SCENE OPENS: Frank is tied to a chair. He is blindfolded. Joey is walking around the chair. He stops and leans in on Frank.

JOEY: How's it going, Frank?

FRANK: What?

JOEY: I said, how's it going?

FRANK: Joey, *(Pause)* is that you?

JOEY: *(JOEY goes over and unties FRANK and takes the blindfold off.)* You're very good, Frank. It didn't even take you two guesses.

FRANK: *(FRANK starts to rise.)* Joey, what the hell's going on here.

JOEY: *(JOEY pushed him back down.)* Hey, what kind of greeting is that? No, "Long time no see?"

FRANK: Cut the bull and tell me what's going on.

JOEY: You know Frank, you ought to get out of that office of yours more. You're really uptight.

FRANK: *(FRANK jumps again.)* Joey, you tell me what's going on or . . .

JOEY: OK, OK, sit down and I'll tell you. *(FRANK continues to stand and he starts to pace.)* Same old Frank, you never change. Well, as I heard it, you *borrowed* a sum of money from a certain person and when that person asked for it back several times, you refused.

FRANK: I don't know what you're talking about. I've got a good job. I don't need to borrow . . .

JOEY: Frank, Frank, please don't. It's so unbecoming when you lie.

FRANK: *(Starting to yell)* I'm not . . . *(He pauses thinking about what he is about to say. He doesn't continue.)*

JOEY: That's better. So, as I was saying, when someone doesn't repay my friend, I'm sent to rectify the situation.

1   FRANK: *(Shocked)* You work for . . .

2   JOEY: Surprise Frank, I got a job. Wouldn't Mom be happy?

3   FRANK: That's not funny.

4   JOEY: I wouldn't think it was funny if I were in your place
5   either.

6   FRANK: So, what have you got to do with all this?

7   JOEY: I told you, I'm here to give you one last chance to give
8   back the money you owe.

9   FRANK: I can't do that. I don't have the money. I already
10   told your boss that.

11   JOEY: I didn't think you did. Well, I guess that simplifies
12   things.

13   FRANK: Meaning what?

14   JOEY: Meaning, I guess I'll have to do my job.

15   FRANK: *(Nervous and annoyed)* Your job? That's a laugh. You
16   said I'd never change. Well, maybe I haven't, but you're
17   even more of a nothing than when you were when we
18   were kids.

19   JOEY: *Shut up and sit down!* *(FRANK sits.)* I want to thank
20   you for that. It makes what I have to do a lot easier, but
21   before I do, there's something I want to say that's been
22   bothering me for a long time.

23   FRANK: Whatever it is, I don't care.

24   JOEY: You should Frank, it concerns you.

25   FRANK: Me?

26   JOEY: Yeah. You see, when I was fourteen and you and that
27   woman kicked me out of the house . . .

28   FRANK: Hold on. First off, nobody kicked you out and
29   secondly, "that woman" happens to be our mother.

30   JOEY: *(Angry)* Your mother, never mine. If I remember
31   correctly, on the last day at home she said, "You're
32   nothing but a punk and always will be." Then what did
33   you, my loyal brother say, "Yeah, why don't you get out
34   of here?"

35   FRANK: Joey, that was nine years ago.

1   JOEY: What difference does it make? I don't remember
2   anyone stopping me then or looking for me since.
3   FRANK: And because of that, you became a murderer?
4   JOEY: You really don't understand, do you? Besides, I'm not
5   a murderer. That's such an ugly word. I prefer to think
6   of it as being a highly trained specialist.
7   FRANK: Specialist. *(Pause)* Mom was right, you did turn out
8   to be a nothing.
9   JOEY: As opposed to what, you?
10   FRANK: Yeah, me. I did fine.
11   JOEY: *(Laughing)* You did pretty well all right. Graduated
12   from college with honors, set up your own accounting
13   firm, got married, *then* you started gambling, embezzling
14   funds, borrowing money. Then your wife, *(He takes out*
15   *some pictures)* started sleeping around. Want to look,
16   Frank? Yeah, you did fine and all in four years.
17   FRANK: *(FRANK leaps from the chair and grabs JOEY by the*
18   *collar.)* You little . . . I ought to . . .
19   JOEY: *(JOEY puts the gun between FRANK'S eyes.)* Kill me?
20   That's highly unlikely Frank, considering the position
21   you're in right now. Sit down, Frank. *(He follows FRANK*
22   *with the gun as he sits.)* I think you ought to know that
23   after I was kicked out of the house I bummed around for
24   a while until I got involved with this group of people.
25   You know, they were the first people who wanted to teach
26   me things.
27   FRANK: Like what, how to kill people?
28   JOEY: No, I started at the bottom, running numbers. Later
29   I was taught how to use this *(Indicates gun)* and how to
30   follow instructions.
31   FRANK: No questions asked?
32   JOEY: That's right.
33   FRANK: That's disgusting.
34   JOEY: Only from your viewpoint. I'm good at what I do and
35   I'm well paid for it. Most importantly though, I'm not in

1   a whole lot of trouble, like you are. So, all in all, who
2   turned out to be the bum?
3   **FRANK:** *(Breaking down on his knees)* **All right Joey, maybe I**
4   **didn't turn out like I thought. You're right I am in trouble,**
5   **but we're still brothers, maybe not close, but we are**
6   **brothers. I need help. I'm begging you for it.**
7   **JOEY:** **I've been waiting for this for nine years. Now the**
8   **success, the good son is asking for help. You know what's**
9   **funny? I'm content. Thank you, Frank.**
10   **FRANK:** **Are you going to help me, Joey?**
11   **JOEY:** *(JOEY picks FRANK up off the floor.)* **Yes, Frank, I am.**
12   **Don't worry, you won't have any more problems.** *(FRANK*
13   *hugs JOEY.)*
14   *(Lights out — Gunshot!)*
15   **END**
16
17
18
19
20
21
22
23
24
25
26
27
28
29
30
31
32
33
34
35

The Politician

CAST: Kate — 40s; Carrie — age open.

SCENE OPENS: Kate is seated at her desk. She is a
congresswoman of the United States. She is looking over some
of her papers. She picks up the phone and pushes the com button.

KATE: **Carrie, would you come in here?** *(Pause)* **Not later,
now.** *(She puts the phone down and goes back to reading. After
a beat there is a knock at the door.)* **Come in.**

CARRIE: *(CARRIE enters. She is KATE'S campaign manager. She
is an ex-lawyer who now works for the congresswoman.)* **Kate,
I just finished that speech for the ladies' club dinner
tomorrow.** *(She gives it to KATE. KATE puts it aside without
looking at it and hands CARRIE some papers.)*

KATE: **Fine. I'll look at it later. Take a look at this.**

CARRIE: **What is it?**

KATE: **Read it and see for yourself.**

CARRIE: *(CARRIE looks over the papers.)* **It's the latest poll
figures. I saw these this morning. What about them?**

KATE: **Read them to me.**

CARRIE: **"The latest Gallop Poll shows incumbent
congresswoman Kate Shaw with fifty-seven percent,
opponent Mary Sands with twenty-four percent.
Nineteen percent are still undecided." Like I said, so?**

KATE: **What do you mean "so"? This is terrible.**

CARRIE: **Terrible? You've got a thirty-three percent lead.
What is so terrible about that?**

KATE: **Here are last months figures. Read them to me.** *(KATE
hands CARRIE some more papers. CARRIE reads.)*

CARRIE: **Let's see . . . last month, Shaw, fifty-seven percent,
Sands, twenty-one percent. OK.**

KATE: **So, look at it! In a month, Mary Sands has gained
three points and I haven't gained any.**

CARRIE: *(Laughing)* **So what? Even if she gained all the rest**

1   of the undecided, which she won't, she still couldn't beat

2   you. Relax, your seat in Congress is safe.

3 KATE: You don't understand, do you? It's not just getting

4   re-elected that's important. It's getting re-elected by the

5   biggest majority that counts.

6 CARRIE: Why?

7 KATE: Should I really have to tell you?

8 CARRIE: Yes, because I don't know what you're so upset

9   about.

10 KATE: I'm upset because it took me a long time to get into

11   Congress and I plan to stay there for a long time. Anytime

12   some opponent starts to make headway and I don't, my

13   strength diminishes and I can't have that, ever! Do you

14   understand what I'm saying?

15 CARRIE: *(Trying to placate her)* Yes, OK, fine. Do me a favor

16   and try to relax. You seem a bit frayed. Don't worry,

17   you're going to beat Mary Sands. *(She starts to exit.)*

18 KATE: Carrie.

19 CARRIE: What? *(She goes back to the desk.)*

20 KATE: I don't want to beat her. I want to crush her.

21 CARRIE: OK, I'll step up the TV and radio spots and I'll

22   schedule some more personal appearances. OK?

23 KATE: Fine. *(CARRIE starts to exit again.)* Carrie, there is one

24   more thing. *(She stops and goes back to the desk again.)*

25 CARRIE: What is it?

26 KATE: To make sure I crush Mary Shaw, I want you to do

27   something with this. *(KATE hands CARRIE an envelope.*

28   *CARRIE opens it and starts to read the contents.)*

29 CARRIE: Where did you get this?

30 KATE: I have my sources.

31 CARRIE: This is a confidential psychiatrist's file.

32 KATE: I know what it is. What do you think we can do with it?

33 CARRIE: Put it back, throw it away, burn it. Those are my

34   first choices.

35 KATE: Oh, come on. If we can leak the fact that Mary Shaw

1   was under psychiatric care, nobody would vote for her,
2   nobody.
3 CARRIE: Yes, but it say's here she was under psychiatric
4   care when she was twenty, for some mild emotional
5   problems, nothing more, and that was a while ago.
6 KATE: So, we don't release all the facts, just enough to hurt.
7 CARRIE: Great, but don't forget a little trick like that could
8   get us sued for libel and defamation of character. I
9   learned about those things when I passed the bar.
10 KATE: Only if it were linked to us, not if it just happened to
11   get out.
12 CARRIE: I don't know why I'm talking about this, because
13   I'm not getting involved with this kind of garbage.
14 KATE: I thought you might say that, so I already took steps
15   and leaked this myself.
16 CARRIE: You didn't? *(Pause)* You did. Well, I'm not going
17   to be a party to this.
18 KATE: Fine.
19 CARRIE: Answer me this, will you?
20 KATE: What?
21 CARRIE: Why is it so important to destroy this woman who
22   has absolutely no chance of winning.
23 KATE: Because I want it known that anyone who comes up
24   against me is going to get hurt.
25 CARRIE: Is this where you say, "Today the Congress,
26   tomorrow the world?" What's happened to you?
27 KATE: What's that supposed to mean?
28 CARRIE: It means, what's happened to that woman I gave
29   up practicing law to help get into Congress eight years
30   ago? Do you know how much I admired you? It was such
31   an honor when you asked me to be on your congressional
32   staff, but I've seen the change and up to three minutes
33   ago I still admired you more than anyone, but that's
34   finished now. I realize that the woman who cared about
35   the issues and the people no longer exists. What's left is a

1   typical politician who cares more about power than
2   anything.
3 KATE: That's right, I do. It is so tough for a woman to rise
4   to political power in this country, so when you get some,
5   you hold on to it for dear life and yes, maybe at the
6   expense of some of your older ideals. But that's the way
7   the game's played and trust me, *I play it well!*
8 CARRIE: Well, I think it stinks.
9 KATE: If you don't like it so much, why don't you just get out!
10 CARRIE: Now, that's the best idea you've had in a long time.
11 *(She starts to exit.)*
12 KATE: Don't think that you're going to find a job with
13   another congressman.
14 CARRIE: I wouldn't want one. You know, you're going to
15   win this election and win big, but in two years time you
16   may find yourself facing a new opponent.
17 KATE: You don't mean you?
18 CARRIE: I didn't say that, but I have learned a lot from you.
19   I know how to win.
20 KATE: You can't be serious?
21 CARRIE: Well, you've got two years to find out. See you. *(She*
22 *exits.)*
23   **END**
24
25
26
27
28
29
30
31
32
33
34
35

PART 3:
MONOLOGS

The Boxer

CAST: Tommy — early 20s.

TOMMY: OK, are there any questions?

INTERVIEWER: Yeah, Tommy. Why do you box?

TOMMY: Why is it that everytime I have a press conference the first question you people ask is, "Tommy, why do you box?" Isn't there anything else you want to know? Anybody? I guess not. You know, one newspaper wanted to know so badly that they hired three psychiatrists to interview me for an article they were doing called, "The Psychology of Boxing." After a week, the first one said that I was masochistic and psychotic, the second one said I had a Napoleonic Complex, and the third one, the one from Vienna, said that because of a lack of attention from my father when I was a kid, I had latent homosexual tendencies, that I compensated for by getting half naked men to beat me up. *(Pause)* That article never came out. If you want to know how I got into boxing, it started when I was a kid. Now, you all may not know it to look at me, but when I was little I was very short. I was, and like a lot of little kids, I got picked on a lot. OK, let's be honest. In the area of New York that I grew up in, the two favorite tourist attractions were the Statue of Liberty and beating up Tommy Parker. Anyway, I was coming home from school one day. It was a typical day — my eye was swollen shut, my nose was bleeding, I was missing a couple of teeth and my old man spots me. Well, he brings me inside, goes out and finds my teeth, stops my nose from bleeding, puts some ice on my eye and looks at me. Then he says to me, me his only son, he says in his best Daddy Walton manner, "Are you going to be a fairy your whole life. Why don't you learn to stand up and fight for yourself? That way you won't come home like a bleeding pansy everyday." Well, with gentle prodding like that, the next day I went out and enrolled in the local 'Y' boxing program, and you know what? I loved it. I loved it so much that I went back everyday for twelve years. And in that twelve years I became the New York State Golden Gloves champion, twice. I won an Olympic silver medal and *now* I am the champion of the world. And you ask me why I box. *(Pause)* For the money!

END

The Adult

CAST: Ali — A high school or college student — age open.

ALI: I know this question has been asked a lot by people my age, but to tell you the truth in my eighteen plus years nobody's ever given me an answer that was half-way intelligent or didn't sound like it was pulled out of some cliché book. So I pose this question to all of you: "When does one become an adult?" Now, before anyone answers, think real hard, because the first person who says, "You'll know" or "When you're twenty-one" is going to hear me scream very loud. OK, with those two gone, does anyone have an answer. *(Pause)* I thought not. I know what the chronological age of adulthood is, but is that really it? My mother thinks it is, but sometimes she can't make up her mind. See what parents like to do is let you be what I call, "an adult of convenience." That means, when it is convenient for them, you're an adult. These times include such things as: babysitting, driving your little brother around, getting a summer job, etc. Now, here comes the interesting part. The minute you want to take the money you made from that job your parents made you get, when they considered you an adult, and spend it on a trip with some of your friends, then no longer are you titled adult, but *young person* or the worst, *young adult* or *child*. By the way, the term *young adult,* that parents throw out, has nothing whatsoever to do with adulthood. They think if they include the word "adult", you'll be pacified. They're wrong. So anyway, where was I? Oh yes, what the determination of adulthood is. I asked my cousin in California what he thought. He's a writer. They always have good advice and he told me, "I don't know," which was not much help, but was the most straightforward answer I got. So, I thought and came up with my own

1	conclusion. See. I figure, if I can look around at the adults
2	in the world and watch them drink, smoke, hurt other
3	people, cheat on their husbands and wives, all those
4	things popular in our society, and decide that they are
5	wrong and that you don't want to do those things, at that
6	moment you are an adult. Which means that there are
7	not many of us around. Think about it!
8	*(Blackout.)*
9	**END**
10	
11	
12	
13	
14	
15	
16	
17	
18	
19	
20	
21	
22	
23	
24	
25	
26	
27	
28	
29	
30	
31	
32	
33	
34	
35	

The Rock Star

CAST: Rock star — age open.

ROCK STAR: I called this press conference because I feel it's about time I cleared some things up. Before any of you ask, I got started about five years ago with some friends, fooling around in my garage. As far as my "meteoric rise to stardom" is concerned, I got lucky. Everyone always thinks that it takes years and years. Well, I've got news for you. It doesn't always. Sure that's the usual way, but there are those cases, where you were playing in the right place at the right time, and you impressed the right person. That's what happened with me and my band. Anyway, I've been hearing a lot of bad things about my band and I want to put a stop to it. I don't know where it's written that if you play Rock and Roll you have to be a drug addict or a slime bucket. I know that in the sixties there was a lot of drug use, but that was then. It's not so much the case now. You know, I'll make a bet that if you look at all those people in our country who are lawyers, you'll find some drugs there too. This really goes for any profession you check into.

As to being a slime bucket, well sometimes we are, but we're only human. You know, I have been linked with everyone in the world. Do you know that last week I was having lunch in Paris with a princess, dinner in Rome with a Hollywood star, and believe it or not, on a tour of China with the band, all at the same time. This was according to one of the more reputable tabloids. The truth is, I was home last week with my wife and *if* she even thought I was doing any of those things, she promised to remove several anatomical parts of my body very painfully. So enough of that.

Now, I'd like to make just one last point. This is

1	to the parents. I know that most of you don't like our
2	music. OK, I don't mind that. Everyone has the right to
3	their opinions, but don't put us down till you listen. You
4	say that we are dangerous, well that's not true. I've
5	listened to some old music where the singers said to,
6	"Beat me Daddy, eight to the bar." This sounds a little
7	masochistic to me, but I never said it should be banned.
8	To each his own. I think all I've wanted to say all along
9	was that we really are good people. Just give us a chance.
10	Oh, by the way, if you still think I'm dangerous, it might
11	make you feel better if you all know that my real name
12	is Marvin Schwartz. How dangerous can I be? Rock on.
13	END
14	
15	
16	
17	
18	
19	
20	
21	
22	
23	
24	
25	
26	
27	
28	
29	
30	
31	
32	
33	
34	
35	

The Eulogy

CAST: Man — age open.
SETTING: A man walks up to a podium. He is dressed in funeral
attire.

MAN: Ladies and gentlemen, I was asked today to say a few
nice words about Harry Giovani. *(Pause)* Harry's *dead.*
That's about as nice as it gets. Now, don't get me wrong,
I don't wish anyone an early demise, but when it comes
to saying something nice about Harry, he's dead is all
that comes to mind. But at this time let's take a look at
the life of this *(Searching for an adjective, but not finding one)*
man.

Harry was always a precocious child. By the time
he was sixteen years of age he ran the largest numbers
racket at Al Capone High. It was here that he met and
established some of his lifelong friendships. Some of
these were: Vinnie the Vice, Slimy Sammy Peters, and
Hank the Butcher. These men all wanted to be here today,
but unfortunately they all have two years left on their
sentences.

His college career was quite auspicious. With the
help of some of his friends, Harry managed to acquire
two degrees from two different universities, three
thousand miles apart at the same time, without ever
going to class. This record has still never been matched
(Pause) or explained.

When Harry grew older his fondness for children
became apparent. He was known for giving large sums
of money to many youth organizations such as: the
Brownies, the Girl Scouts of America, the YWCA and the
Sunshine Girls. He liked helping these children and
enjoyed having many pictures taken with them. *(He
reaches into his pocket and pulls out some pictures.)* **As a matter**

1	of fact, here are some of them. Here's one with little Mary
2	and one with little Suzie and one with Troup 337. I would
3	love to share the rest with you, but these are the only
4	ones not confiscated by the FBI.
5	As far as business went, Harry was generous to a
6	fault with his clients. And there was no problem if you
7	faulted with Harry's generosity. You never heard from
8	him again. Of course no one ever heard from you again,
9	but that's business.
10	As a family man, no one could top Harry. This can
11	be proved if you talk to any of Harry's twelve widows.
12	He would have made things easier if he had divorced
13	one, before marrying another, but that was Harry.
14	And finally, when Harry found out that his time
15	was near, he decided not to quit. He was a fighter as he
16	proved by his two-day stand-off with fourteen law
17	enforcement agencies. Finally though, he had to succumb
18	to the pressure *(Pause)* and 13,000 rounds of ammunition.
19	So in closing, Harry, if death is anything like your
20	life we will all tread softly and speak softly because you
21	will always be below our feet, watching.
22	END
23	
24	
25	
26	
27	
28	
29	
30	
31	
32	
33	*NOTE: The numerals running vertically down the left margin*
34	*of each page of dialog are for the convenience of the director.*
35	*With these he/she may easily direct attention to a specific passage.*

ABOUT THE AUTHOR
Garry Kluger

Garry Kluger started acting in theatre at age eight and it has been a never-ceasing activity through all of his school years. Sports, especially gymnastic events, occupied whatever free time his college days permitted beyond acting. His career path has never wavered since his early days in Baltimore, Maryland where he was born. In high school and college he won many top awards in drama events. Since moving to the entertainment capital of Los Angeles, he has won many auditions for feature films and TV shows. He has appeared in starring as well as supporting roles in film, TV and off-Broadway shows including both popular and classic plays.

Garry's versatility extends beyond acting and sports. In addition to his theatrical and musical skills, he has found a special niche for his writing talent. There had been a critical shortage of original short scenes for actors who wanted to "showcase" for network casting directors and film producers. Garry wrote his own scenes to fill this need. Now professional actors at entertainment centers nationwide are asking for Garry's auditions. This collection of audition scenes was published in direct response to this need.

NOTES:

NOTES:

NOTES:

NOTES:

If you have found this book of audition scenes to be helpful, we believe you will also find these books to be of value to you:

WINNING MONOLOGS FOR YOUNG ACTORS

by PEG KEHRET

"These monologs will satisfy young peoples' needs for audition/classroom drama material."
— booklist

Honest-to-life characterizations to delight actors and audiences of all ages

For speech contests, acting exercises, auditions or audience entertainment in a stage review, these short monologs are to theatre what Art Buchwald is to journalism. Warm. Funny. And best of all — real! Sixty-five characterizations for girls, boys and both together. *Sample titles include:* **First Date; I'm Not My Brother, I'm Me; My Blankee; The Driver's Test Is a Piece of Cake** *and* **Cafeteria Lunches.** Any young person will relate to the topics of these scripts. The only book of "nontheatrical" monologs we know of.

57 ORIGINAL AUDITIONS FOR ACTORS

by EDDIE LAWRENCE
introduction by JASON ROBARDS

A workbook of monologs for professional and nonprofessional actors

Any actor, professional or would-be professional will enjoy the many characterization challenges this book offers. It's a virtual treasure-house of interesting types staged in mini-play monolog format — **Movie Siren, Taxi Driver, Delinquent, Folk Singer, Old Vaudevillian, Waitress, Flim-Flam Man** — these and many, many more! For the actor, it's a living picture gallery of drama. A wonderful library of characters for study and practice. Each audition is about two minutes long. A book for every actor's bookshelf and suitcase.

Both of these paperback books are available at bookstores or from Meriwether Publishing Ltd., P.O. Box 7710, Colorado Springs, Colorado 80933

ORDER FORM

MERIWETHER PUBLISHING LTD.
P.O. BOX 7710
COLORADO SPRINGS, CO 80933
TELEPHONE: (303)594-4422

Please send me the following books:

_____ **Original Audition Scenes for Actors #BB-B129** $9.95
by Garry Michael Kluger
A book of professional-level dialogs and monologs

_____ **Stage Lighting in the Boondocks #BB-B141** $5.95
by James Hull Miller
A simplified guide to stage lighting

_____ **Self-Supporting Scenery #BB-B105** $8.95
by James Hull Miller
A scenic workbook for the open stage

_____ **One-Act Plays for Acting Students #BB-B159** $14.95
by Dr. Norman A. Bert
An anthology of complete one-act plays

_____ **57 Original Auditions for Actors #BB-B181** $6.95
by Eddie Lawrence
A workbook of monologs for actors

_____ **Theatre Games for Young Performers #BB-B188** $7.95
by Maria C. Novelly
Improvisations and exercises for developing acting skills

_____ **Winning Monologs for Young Actors #BB-B127** $7.95
by Peg Kehret
Honest-to-life monologs for young actors

I understand that I may return any book
for a full refund if not satisfied.

NAME: _____

ORGANIZATION NAME: _____

ADDRESS: _____

CITY: _____ STATE: _____ ZIP: _____

PHONE: _____

☐ **Check Enclosed**
☐ **Visa or Master Card #** _____

Signature: _____
(required for Visa/Mastercard orders)

COLORADO RESIDENTS: Please add 3% sales tax.
SHIPPING: Include $1.50 for the first book and 50¢ for each additional book ordered.

☐ *Please send me a copy of your complete catalog of books or plays.*